CROSSING THE RACIAL DIVIDE

Close Friendships Between Black and White Americans

Kathleen Odell Korgen

PRAEGER

Westport, Connecticut
London

Library of Congress Cataloging-in-Publication Data

Korgen, Kathleen Odell, 1967–
    Crossing the racial divide : close friendships between Black and White Americans /
Kathleen Odell Korgen.
        p. cm.
    Includes bibliographical references and index.
    ISBN 0–275–97281–X (alk. paper)
    1. United States—Race relations. 2. Friendship—United States. I. Title.

E185.625 .K647 2002
305.8′00973—dc21   2002072548

British Library Cataloguing in Publication Data is available.

Library of Congress Catalog Card Number: 2002072548
ISBN: 0–275–97281–X

First published in 2002

Praeger Publishers, 88 Post Road West, Westport, CT 06881
An imprint of Greenwood Publishing Group, Inc.
www.praeger.com

Printed in the United States of America

The paper used in this book complies with the
Permanent Paper Standard issued by the National
Information Standards Organization (Z39.48–1984).

10 9 8 7 6 5 4 3 2 1

This book is dedicated to my mother, Patricia Odell, and the memory of my father, Walter Tomkins Odell.

Contents

Acknowledgments

As I researched and wrote this book, I was heartened to read Mary Waters's acknowledgments in *Black Identities: West Indian Immigrant Dreams and American Realities.*[1] She writes there that "when I try to write I am productive and enjoy the process about 5 percent of the time. The other 95 percent is pretty miserable."

While I would not presume to compare myself to Mary Waters on any other level, it gave me some consolation during my own struggles with *Crossing the Racial Divide* to know that writing a book can be difficult for even the most prominent writers in the field. I can even safely say that I had more fun writing this book than Mary Waters did writing hers!

I had much to be thankful for in the process of creating *Crossing the Racial Divide.* I cannot imagine writing this book without the help, encouragement, love, and overall support of my husband, Jeff. As always, he was my best friend, first editor, coach, and cheerleader throughout. My daughter, Julie, was as understanding as any infant and toddler can be of the time I devoted to this book. Her sister, Jessica, cooperated admirably by staying in the womb until I finished the manuscript.

I was also blessed with the support of many other family members, friends, colleagues, and those who were once relative strangers (but are now friends). Patricia Odell, the best, most reliable mother, grandmother, and professional colleague, commented on early drafts and located interviewees for me. John Odell also gave me good advice on the text and directed me to interviewees. He really deserves to have his name in large type. Michael Odell, Ann Odell, Conor Odell, and Judy and Ben Korgen gave me much needed encouragement and enjoyable time away from this project. I also owe a debt of gratitude to many colleagues who commented on drafts of the book. Mark Ellis, Lou Gaydosh, Howard Lune, Jim Mahon, Patrick McManimon, Eileen O'Brien, and Peter Stein all provided useful suggestions for making the book stronger. One of my students, Ani Desilets, contributed research assistance.

Some of the greatest pleasures I had in writing this book were the opportunities provided for renewing old friendships and making new ones as I traveled across the country interviewing people. Mark Brinkmoeller opened up his apartment to me and my family and was an invaluable resource in finding interviewees. He also became a great friend. Susan Engels, a mere acquaintance before I began this project, also provided interviewees, a place to stay, and, best of all, a wonderful new friendship. Alex, Denise, Gabrielle, and Gemma del Carmen provided friendship and sustenance when I was far from home. During my all-too brief "catch up" visits with them, MaryAnne Lynn and Marie Elena Gioiella made me remember and appreciate just how great it is to have 3:00 A.M. friends. Peter Stein and Michele Murdock gave me encouragement and helped locate interviewees. Tom Chabolla, Barbara McCarthy, Phyllis Schumacher, and Lillian Wall all went out of their way to assist me in finding and setting up interviews.

My editor, Suzanne Staszak-Silva, was both supportive and extremely helpful in her feedback. She successfully prodded me to expand where necessary and to avoid many pitfalls throughout. I am very fortunate to have her as my editor. I also appreciate the comments of the three anonymous reviewers hired by Praeger.

Finally, I must thank the interviewees themselves. This book is based on their stories. It could not have been written without their generosity and experience as members of close friendships formed across the greatest racial divide in the United States.

NOTE

1. Mary C. Waters, *Black Identities: West Indian Immigrant Dreams and American Realities* (Cambridge: Harvard University Press, 1999), p. vii.

Introduction

As I traveled the country conducting interviews for this book, I encountered evidence of the division that remains between most white and black Americans in some unexpected places. Shortly after flying into the Dallas/Fort Worth airport, I stopped at a fast-food restaurant for lunch before my first interview in the area. A public school was across the street, and I soon found myself one of two adults in a restaurant that seemed overflowing with young teenagers of different racial and ethnic backgrounds, particularly white, black, and Latino. There was no obvious self-segregation of the youth by race/ethnicity. The other adult, an elderly woman, and I looked at each other and laughed as we ate surrounded by what seemed to be increasingly noisy teenagers. She then leaned over to me and said, "You know, I still can't get used to it, seeing them together like this."

This woman in the fast-food restaurant continued, speaking disapprovingly of the racial intermingling we witnessed. She might easily be dismissed as a remnant of an earlier time, when segregation was the rule. It would be nice to end this story by saying that this woman has simply not adjusted to a society in which interracial friendships are common. However, this is not the case. While her attitude may not be voiced often today, the reality is that the lunch crowd we were surrounded by was exceptional in their cross-racial interactions. Few Americans have the opportunity to become accustomed to seeing blacks and whites with one another.

Close to four decades after the culmination of the civil rights movement, we are still separated from one another "by the color of our skin," as Leonard Steinhorn and Barbara Diggs-Brown say in the title of their book.[1] Close friendships between blacks and whites are still a rarity. This division prevents the United States from realizing much of its potential strength.

In our increasingly racially and ethnically diverse society, the ability to form cross-racial and cross-cultural relationships is vital for the well-being and stability of the nation. If we are to work together effectively, we must understand one another. We must be capable of seeing society from the perspective of other races, as well as our own. Close cross-racial friendships grant us exposure to different ways of viewing the world and make us more adept at living in a racially diverse nation. They also benefit us on an individual level.

Paula Rothenberg, one of the founders of multicultural studies, vividly describes the absence of such friendships in her own early life in her autobiographical book, *Invisible Privilege*.[2] Raised in an upper-middle-class white neighborhood bordering Manhattan's Central Park, Rothenberg's only interactions with black people were with the maids her mother employed. She grew up in one of the most racially diverse cities in the world yet, like almost all her peers, socialized only with whites. It was not until she was an adult, researching and teaching on sexism and racism, that she realized "one of the least recognized costs of racism is the loss of so many unrealized friendships."

In *My First White Friend*,[3] black journalist Patricia Raybon described how her memories of a brief high school friendship with a white person enabled her to eventually stop spending energy "hating white people." As a teenager starting at a new, predominantly white school she began to develop a friendship with a white classmate. However, Raybon quickly abandoned her cross-racial friendship when she began to form relationships with black classmates in her school. Memories of that cross-racial friendship remained with her, though. In her forties, Raybon was able to look back on that brief high school friendship and recognize that love and friendship across the divide between white and black Americans is both possible and necessary. Knowing that such friendships were possible, Raybon could start the process of unwrapping herself from the racial hatred she had carried with her and begin to cross the racial divide.

Just as Raybon's childhood cross-racial friendship enabled her to see goodness across the racial divide, the friendships of those interviewed in this book have encouraged each friend to develop a more positive attitude toward members of the other race. They provide examples of how friendships can form across the racial divide and the effect these relationships have on their members' views on racial issues. To differing degrees, these whites and blacks, like Raybon, have all grown through experiencing cross-racial friendships.

It took Raybon more than four decades to come to the realization that Americans must make personal connections across racial lines in order to "start living up to our collective and individual potential as a blessed human community."[4] Most white and black Americans, however, never experience such relationships. Few close black/white friendships exist. To use Raybon's words, American society has not yet come close to "living up to [its] . . . potential."

The United States is still racially segregated. Few whites and blacks live in the same neighborhood or attend the same classes in school. The opportunity for the development of close cross-racial friends simply does not exist for most Americans.

Every racial group in the United States has its own unique history and set of issues. Every nonwhite race has faced discrimination at the hands of white Americans. While today rates of prejudice and aversion between whites and blacks are higher than those between whites and other nonwhite racial minorities, all have faced severe discrimination and continue to deal with unequal treatment. American Indians endured genocide. Some Asian Americans lived in concentration camps. Latinos, an ethnic group often mistaken for a distinct race, have also had to endure the hardships of land seizures, stifling poverty, and deportations.

Each group has its own, distinct, relationship with white Americans and other Americans of color. It makes sense, therefore, to examine only one type of cross-racial friendship at a time. This book focuses on close friendships between black and white Americans. In doing so, the following chapters examine

1. the barriers between blacks and whites

2. how close black-white friendships form despite these obstacles

3. the influence of race on the friendships

4. how the friendship affects each friend's views on racial issues

5. the social structures that impede the development of cross-racial friendships

6. the potential benefits to society of bridging the divide between white and black Americans

OUTLINE OF BOOK

Chapter 1 puts the study of close black-white friendships into context. It provides an overview of such cross-racial friendships in the United States and discusses the perspectives of those who maintain that differences exist between whites and blacks and those who either do not believe in or try to dismiss dissimilarities between the races. In doing so, it answers the question, Are blacks and whites "opposites"?

Blacks and whites have virtually the same genetic makeup. However, the two races have social and historical differences. Persons who maintain a "colorblind" perspective tend to ignore or minimize these differences. The colorblind approach leads many people, at both ends of the political spectrum, to believe that the playing field between whites and blacks is even today, when, in reality, whites have far more privileges than blacks in our society.

In chapter 2, the focus turns to close cross-racial friendships that currently exist. It compares the development of these friendships with typical, same-race friendship formation and examines the different reactions that whites and blacks, in general, have to close black-white friendships. While whites are more likely to look favorably on platonic cross-racial friendships than blacks, they are primarily responsible for the institutional divide that prevents the formation of many such friendships. Chapter 2 also provides a discussion about the relationship between culture and race.

How do close black/white friends deal with the issue of race? Chapter 3 illustrates the three primary ways that cross-racial friends handle race in their relationships. While the most common means is avoidance, some use humor to deal with the issue, and others confront the topic of race directly, in serious discussions.

Issues of race threatened the friendship of only one pair of interviewees. The experience of this pair of friends helps to reveal the importance of establishing the firm foundation of a friendship before delving into the volatile topic of race. Their experience indicates that those who do talk about racial issues with one another must tread carefully and ensure that race does not become the centerpiece of their relationship. Only one-fourth of the friends seriously discussed racial issues with their close cross-racial friends.

Chapter 4 takes a closer look at the friendship pairs who avoid the issue of race. It uses the social psychological concept of homophily to make sense of this popular means of handling racial issues in this type of friendship. It also reveals the different perspectives of white and black interviewees on the topic.

Most whites would like to believe that they and their black friends have equal opportunities. Their desire to see their black friends as similar to themselves often prevents them from recognizing racism and their own racial privilege. Most blacks, on the other hand, recognize racism but absolve their white friends from blame for the race-based advantages they have.

How close black-white friendships influence each friend's views on race is the primary focus of chapter 5. Every friend's attitudes about race and members of the other race changed because of the cross-racial friendship. However, these changes run a gamut of intensity and differ between the races.

All the white friends expressed greater empathy for blacks and a broader perspective on racial issues. Whites, in general, were more likely to view other blacks as potential friends because of their close cross-racial friendships. Blacks, too, expressed more positive attitudes toward whites as a result of their close friendships with white people. One-fourth of the black interviewees said that their close cross-racial friendships allowed them to recognize that there are some good white people.

Chapter 6 focuses on how we, as a society, might bridge the institutional racial divide. In doing so, it describes the institutional impediments to interracial friendships and provides relative success stories in the endeavor to alleviate the institutional separation of the races. It focuses on the institutional divide in housing and schools and includes a description of the benefits to society of dismantling these socially constructed divisions between white and black Americans. Shaker Heights, Ohio; West Mount Airy, Philadelphia; and several universities are provided as examples of successful efforts to bridge the racial divide in these institutions.

The conclusion summarizes the main points of the book and argues that crossing the racial divide will make our nation stronger. We must appreciate and learn from the close cross-racial friendships that now exist. However, we must also recognize the institutional barriers that remain in the way of larger numbers of black/white friendships and work to alleviate them. Once we take these steps, we can see both the extent of the divide and the means to cross it.

NOTES

1. Leonard Steinhorn and Barbara Diggs-Brown, *By the Color of Our Skin: The Illusion of Integration and the Reality of Race* (New York: Plume, 2000).

2. Paula Rothenberg, *Invisible Privilege: A Memoir About Race, Class, and Gender* (Lawrence: University Press of Kansas, 2000).

3. Patricia Raybon, *My First White Friend: Confessions on Race, Love, and Forgiveness* (New York: Penguin, 1996).

4. Raybon, *My First White Friend*, p. 136.

Are Blacks and Whites "Opposites"?

I don't know one black person that lives in the town [where I grew up].
It's a completely white town. . . . Sometimes [black] people come to the
beach. . . . But you know they're from a different town because they come
in like a bus. Like a school bus . . . for a field trip.

Pete, white, 21

Blacks go to Pete's all-white New England hometown of Shoreham only on
field trips. That may sound extreme, but it is not unusual. There are thousands
of all-white neighborhoods and towns across the country, most without a beach
or similar attraction that would draw people in from out of town. Many white
children from such towns have never had a conversation with a black person.
In fact, it is common for white students leaving such areas to enter colleges
with 90 percent white student bodies and feel surprised by the "incredible"
diversity on campus.

Most black and white Americans live in almost completely separate worlds.
While the U.S. population has become more racially and ethnically diverse,
whites and blacks still tend to live apart. According to a 2001 study by Albany
University's Mumford Center for Comparative Urban and Regional Research,[1]
the typical white person lives in a neighborhood that is 83 percent white and
only 7 percent black, while the average black citizen resides in an area that is
more than 50 percent black and only 33 percent white.

Sandra Sayles,[2] a fifty-year-old black professor at a large southern university,
vividly described the racial separation evident in the Chicago neighborhood in
which she grew up.

In my twenties, we had a dog that we obtained when he was about three weeks old.
Living in the city of Chicago, all of our neighbors were black and the community was
black. . . . One afternoon I was sitting on the sofa. The dog was in the backyard, and
the dog was barking like crazy. I couldn't figure out what was going on. So I went out
into the yard and there was a meter reader coming to read the electric meters on the
houses. The dog was trying all it could to get over the fence into the neighbor's yard,
where the meter reader was. I thought for a minute; I thought, now what is going on?

They read the meter once a month. The dog sees meter readers every month. Why is he so upset today? It finally dawned on me, the meter reader was white. It was atypical for us to have a white meter reader. As I thought back, I didn't think the dog had ever seen a white person. And, so even in the dog's eyes, this was something unusual and something where the dog felt the need to protect the family and the houses around him. (Sandra, black, 50)

Close to three decades later, Sandra still notices, in various places she goes, that blacks and whites rarely interact with one another.

At times I'll be out in the street and I'll see white children, a year or two years old, and they will just stare at me. I'll even have times when if I get near the kid they'll run to their parents crying. That says to me they've probably never seen a black person before. (Sandra, black, 50)

Just like the dog feared the white meter reader, the white children feared Sandra because they had never seen anyone who looked like her before. She is an unusual sight, and thus alarming to them.

However, it would be hard to discover the separation that exists between the races by reading the newspaper or watching television today. A June 1999 *Boston Globe* headline announced that "The Newest Bostonians are Multi-racial, Multicultural, and Pleased to Meet You."[3] Polls across the United States indicate that increasing numbers of blacks and whites are becoming friends. According to a May 2000 *Boston Globe* poll, 87 percent of blacks and 86 percent of whites report having friends of another race. Eighty-four percent of blacks and 77 percent of whites say that they have eaten in the home of a person of another race.[4] In Seattle, "fry dinners" bring whites and blacks to the same supper tables all over the city.[5] President George W. Bush's cabinet is more racially and ethnically diverse than was that of President William J. Clinton, who proclaimed that he was going to create a cabinet that "looked like America" and came closer to achieving that goal than any previous President. *Any Day Now*, a show about a black and a white woman who are best friends, is a hit on the Lifetime channel. The acclaimed 1994 movie *Pulp Fiction* starred a white and a black man in the leading roles. The multiracially cast movie *The Fast and the Furious* became, for a short time, the number-one movie in June 2001 as the *Los Angeles Times* declared that the "studios have only begun to catch up with the colorblind nature of today's MTV generation."[6]

Clearly, many Americans would like to believe that race relations are improving and that friendships across racial lines are becoming common. This optimistic viewpoint breaks down under scrutiny. According to the latest available National Opinion Research Center data, both white and black Americans prove to be more optimistic than accurate in their descriptions of their personal race relations. When asked whether they had close black friends, 42.1 percent of whites said yes, they did. However, when asked to first write down the names of their closest friends and *then* identify their races, only 6 percent of whites listed a black person as one of those friends.[7] Approximately 62 percent of blacks maintained that they had a close white friend when asked but only 15.2 percent included a white person in their list of close friends. In fact, Fayneese Miller, the director of the Center for the Study of Race and Ethnicity in America at Brown University, maintains that interracial friendships are actually no more prevalent in the United States than they are in the recently desegregated South Africa.[8]

Indeed, it would be surprising if large numbers of close friendships between black and white Americans did exist. In light of the social sciences' widely accepted understanding of interpersonal attraction, interracial friendships are abnormal. Social psychologists have found that people are most likely to become friends or romantic partners with people who are similar to themselves.[9] People also tend to like people they believe will like them.[10] This aspect of attraction reinforces the effects of similarity promoting interpersonal attraction.

The strong influence of perceived similarities on friendship formation makes cross-racial friendships unlikely. Like sex and gender, race has traditionally been referred to as an ascribed characteristic of identity that is immutable[11] and divisive.[12] The idea that people are attracted to those like themselves and the notion that racial differences are divisive has thwarted many attempts to make sense of interracial friendships within existing friendship theories.

The classical literature in the area of friendship and identity, combined with the starkly realistic NORC data, would seem to quash optimists who maintain that race does not impede the development of friendships. However, close friendships between black and white Americans do exist, and while still relatively small in number, they appear to be on the rise. In light of these conflicting messages, we must reanalyze the phenomenon of interracial friendships by studying existing friendships between persons traditionally viewed as racial "opposites"—blacks and whites.

"COLORBLINDNESS" VERSUS DIFFERENCES BETWEEN BLACK AND WHITE

Are blacks and whites really "opposites"? In the nineteenth century, scholars supported the notion that genetic differences between blacks and whites made slavery ethically justifiable. One such scholar was Samuel Cartwright, the chair of a committee of the Medical Association of Louisiana brought together to provide an account of the "diseases and physical peculiarities of the Negro race." The committee maintained that slavery was ethically just, as it benefited blacks "in body, mind and morals."[13] This type of scientific racism resulted in consistent "scholarly" findings of black physical and mental inferiority and perceived dangers to the white race from any interracial mixing.[14]

Today, few still argue that any race is biologically superior or inferior to another.[15] The Human Genome Project has demonstrated convincingly that, biologically, "all humans share the same basic set of genes."[16] The legal and social definitions of the term *race* have changed from age to age and from society to society. A trip to another nation, like Cuba,[17] reveals differences in the notions of race. The loud debate over racial classifications in the 2000 Census made it clear that official racial categorizations have varied throughout the history of the United States. Sociologists studying race relations in the United States now generally use the term *race* to "refer to the common social distinctions made on the basis of physical appearance."[18]

Most Americans today racially classify people they meet from their phenotypes and skin coloring.[19] However, only approximately .01 percent of our genes shape our external appearance. Even variances in occurrences of diseases among different racial groups, such as relatively high numbers of African Americans developing sickle-cell anemia, can be traced back to the alteration of a single gene. Like darkness in skin pigmentation, sickle-cell anemia developed as a result of certain climactic conditions that fostered natural selection. Both darker skin and the genetic trait that predisposes populations to sickle-cell anemia were survival advantages. While effective in preventing malaria, the unfortunate by-product of the change in the single gene was a greater likelihood that some African Americans will have sickle-cell anemia, which can be fatal. Other differences in health between races, such as relatively high rates of high blood pressure among African American males, can be traced to disparities in economic and social conditions.[20]

On the other hand, human attributes such as intelligence, artistic ability, and social prowess, which vary inside populations, are affected by thousands, perhaps tens of thousands, of the approximately 80,000 genes each human possesses. There is no longer any doubt that the overwhelming majority of gene variation occurs within, rather than between, racial groups.[21] The population of any town, anywhere in the world, represents the vast majority of variation within the human species. In other words, those who wish to explore genetic differences between people will find greater variety within rather than beyond racial borders. The genetic differences between races are, in the words of geneticist Mary-Claire King, "quite literally superficial."[22]

However, simply because race is a social, rather than a biological, construction does not mean that differences do not exist between groups socially labeled as distinct races. Different groups have used the notion of cultural differences between races to argue the superiority of "their" race for years. When Social Darwinism was discredited in the early part of the twentieth century, many simply replaced culture for genes in their arguments "demonstrating" why whites are superior to blacks.[23] On the other hand, some Afrocentrists, stressing the preeminence of blacks, maintain that some of the greatest achievements of Western culture, such as Greek philosophy, the "harnessing" of electricity, and the field of aerodynamics, actually originated in Africa.[24]

While a broad range of groups from Afrocentrists to affirmative-action proponents to multiculturalists and cultural Darwinists maintain that there are differences—historic and cultural—between blacks and whites that continue to distinguish these racial groups, a new perspective on race is rapidly gaining popularity. Many Americans now maintain that there are no real dissimilarities between blacks and whites. In line with this viewpoint, more and more Americans are declaring themselves "colorblind."

Colorblindness

If you are white, it is hard to avoid the message that race should no longer be important in our society. As Benjamin DeMott pointed out in 1995,[25] white and black movie characters do not address or confront issues of race, and in early-twenty-first-century movies popular with white Americans—such as *Swordfish, Ocean's 11, Scream 2,* and *Pearl Harbor*—the observation is still true. Instead, the emphasis is on "revealing their common humanity." In tandem with this popular portrayal of blacks and whites, proponents of colorblindness say that we should learn to avoid noticing racial differences because they are, in the end, truly meaningless. Throughout these stories in the popular media, the implicit moral argument concerning race is clear. If all Americans could just learn to be "colorblind," and not see race, we could recognize our sameness and become friends.

Conservative Americans are increasingly using the concept of colorblindness in their language. For instance, many right-wing politicians and pundits, such as Newt Gingrich, Darvit Horowitz, George Will, and Charles Krauthammer, have quoted Martin Luther King Jr.'s statement that we should "be judged by the content of [our] character rather than the color of [our] skin" in their arguments against affirmative-action programs.[26] Abigail and Stephan Thernstrom, two of the most vocal opponents of affirmative action, use selected pieces of Dr. King's statement in their book *America in Black and White: One Nation, Indivisible.*[27]

Many liberals also argue in favor of "colorblind" policies. These advocates of colorblindness tend to believe that if we act as if race does not matter, it will not matter. Jeff Hitchock, while an advocate of a multiracial/multicultural perspective himself, points out in *Unraveling the White Cocoon* that "the idea of colorblindness has become the orthodox view among most Americans." As Hitchcock describes it, colorblindness "stands against racial categorization, upholds individuality, emphasizes our common humanity, and works toward achieving 'one people' status."[28] More and more Americans, in opposition to racial discrimination on the one hand and race-based preferences on the other, believe that the solution to racial problems is colorblindness.

Believers in colorblindness look forward to a time when race becomes not just inconsequential, but also overlooked. Proponents of colorblindness argue that race is meaningless and should be treated as both irrelevant and nonexistent (sometimes people espousing colorblindness will, confusingly, try to make both points at the same time). They maintain that blacks and whites should be viewed, described, and treated simply as individuals rather than members of particular races. Unlike opponents of colorblindness who acknowl-edge racial features and the different impact race has on whites and blacks, adherents to colorblindness maintain that they never think about race when forming friendships. While both colorblind proponents and opponents may be much more interested in a friend's personality than skin color, colorblind ad-vocates maintain that they do not even notice the race of a cross-racial friend.

Proponents of colorblindness argue that social science has not caught up to the changing times. In fact, many say that social scientists, by studying issues of race, are actually perpetuating racism in our society, and, therefore, prevent greater social interaction between the races by giving credence to the notion that race matters. If true, it would not be the first time social scientists have been accused of espousing some seemingly dated modes of thinking. For in-stance, it has only been in the last few years that psychologists and sociologists have begun to portray mixed-race children as anything but doomed to be nega-tively "marginalized" and "confused."[29] In addition, only since the Multi-cultural Movement and the second wave of the Women's Movement (1970s) have social scientists felt compelled to move beyond a sample of white male college students in studies of human behavior.

However, despite its historically white male bias, social science has proved invaluable in helping us to understand how our society works and recognize the injustices that may seem like routine aspects of its operation. For instance, the law upholding "separate but equal" conditions as constitutional in *Plessy v. Ferguson* might not have been overturned through *Brown v. Board of Edu-cation* without Kenneth Clark's doll experiment that revealed black children's feelings of inferiority to whites.[30] For almost the last quarter-century, social scientists have repeatedly proven the need for enforcement of the Fair Housing Act.[31] The benefits of affirmative-action programs in colleges (discussed in chapter 6) are among the latest useful social scientific discoveries concerning race.[32] It is only through research in the social sciences that we can begin to understand what drives members of different races apart and what can unite them. Examining close friendships between blacks and whites enables us to comprehend how friendships can form across the racial divide and the influence of those friendships on the individual friends and society.

Differences Between Black and White

Social scientists argue that we cannot just "wish away" tensions and dis-parities between black and white Americans. Despite the best intentions of many of those who see themselves as "colorblind," the notion of blacks and whites as *social* "opposites" in the social sciences has much good research be-hind it. In studies performed throughout the history of the study of prejudice in the United States, results indicated that whites are consistently less willing to interact with blacks than with other racial and ethnic groups.[33] Since such research was conducted in the 1950s, when given a choice, whites have shown a clear preference to work with, reside next to, and intermarry with Asians or Hispanics rather than blacks.

The physical distance between American blacks and whites noted earlier parallels the social distance between them. The residential segregation that leads to few blacks growing up around whites and even fewer whites growing up among blacks impedes other opportunities for cross-racial interaction. As Steinhorn and Diggs-Brown describe in *By the Color of Our Skin*, "where we live defines so much of our lives—how we get to work, where our kids go to school, where we shop, whom we chat with, and who our friends will be."[34] Repeated studies indicate that the more people are exposed to members of other races in their neighborhoods and schools as youths, the more accepting they will be of other races and likely to have cross-racial friendships when they become adults.[35]

Today, most cross-racial communication takes place within hierarchical, rather than friendship, relationships. In a 1999 study, Hudson and Hines-Hudson distinguished between the effects of interaction that takes place between whites and blacks in friendships and in work and school situations, where whites are often in positions of dominance. They found that, in the latter settings, "familiarity" can actually breed "contempt" and resentment rather than the greater understanding and respect common among relationships based on friendship. While interactions in friendship situations can lead to positive interracial relations, Hudson and Hines-Hudson caution that "the [negative] influence of power relations mediated through social and economic institutions [on race relations] cannot be discounted."[36] While friendships spark mutual trust and admiration, most blacks and whites are not friends. Those who do communicate with one another usually interact in nonfriendly, hierarchical settings. According to antiracism expert Eileen O'Brien, colorblindness is a means for the "majority of white Americans" to avoid acknowledging these facts and "justify their lack of support for any further policy solutions for race related problems."[37]

While many of those who maintain that there are differences between whites and blacks are white power advocates or black separatists, most are neither. Many whites and blacks, while advocating equality and integration of the races, say that we must acknowledge and learn to deal with real differences between whites and blacks in the United States. Opponents of colorblindness maintain that one should, for instance, be able to recognize and feel comfortable acknowledging racial features when describing a friend of another race. As Barbara, an eighty-four-year-old white interviewee, observes,

You know . . . when you thought you really had reached a point [in your interracial friendships] when you could say "I don't notice if they're black or white," at some [point] you say to yourself "Hey! If you don't notice that, you're not recognizing them at all!" You know, ah, that's part of who they are, their color, just like their hair or your eyes or anything else. So, to me, that was something that I, that was a kind of a moment where I began to take another look, you know. It wasn't enough just to say, well, I don't even notice if they're black or white. Well, of course I do! Because that's part of how they look, you know. But I think that's just maturing [laughs]. (Barbara, white, 84)

Implicit, but not recognized by those who promote colorblindness, is the notion that whiteness is normalized. The colorblind norm is that it is okay to describe a white person as having red, curly, shoulder-length hair, but not acceptable to notice the color, texture, or length of a black person's hair.

Many blacks who believe in racial differences are insulted at the idea that a white person would not notice or, worse, try not to notice their blackness. They see their physical features as aspects of themselves to be proud of rather than aspects that should be ignored, as if they were unsightly or insulting to mention. Lena Williams, in *It's the Little Things*, relates a story about a white colleague who mentioned at a diversity meeting that he does not see color and only sees "people as people"; several blacks at the meeting took offense. One black colleague asked him, "But don't you see how offensive that sounds when you take away a vital part of a person's identity?" He didn't. Williams suggests that "take the same observation and replace the word *color* with *gender* or *age* and maybe you'll get the point." Williams notes that most women would resent it if people with whom they interact maintain that they do not notice their gender.[38]

These individual debates over colorblindness relate to how people view the social inequities between the races. Blacks and whites who advocate affirmative-action programs maintain that the historical and structural injustices that remain as obstacles for persons of color require us to recognize that blacks face a disadvantage in our society due to their race. Not providing some assistance for blacks now would be wrong. Benjamin DeMott forcefully argues that advocates of colorblindness lose "touch with the two fundamental truths of race in America; namely that because of what happened in the past, blacks and whites cannot yet be the same; and that because what happened in the past was no mere matter of ill will or insult, it is not reparable by one-on-one goodwill."[39]

President Bill Clinton echoed DeMott's position in his 1995 speech on affirmative action when he related the following:

The unemployment rate for African Americans remains about twice that of whites. The Hispanic rate is still much higher. . . . According to the recently completed Glass Ceiling Report, sponsored by Republican members of Congress, in the nation's largest companies only six-tenths of one percent of senior management positions are held by African Americans, four-tenths of a percent by Hispanic Americans, three-tenths of a percent by Asian Americans. . . . Just last week, the Chicago Federal Reserve Bank reported that black home loan applicants are more than twice as likely to be denied credit as whites with the same qualifications; and that Hispanic applicants are more than one and a half times as likely to be denied loans as whites with the same qualifications. . . . Evidence abounds in other ways of the persistence of the kind of bigotry that can affect the way we think even if we're not conscious of it, in hiring and promotion and business and educational decisions.[40]

Joe Feagin's 2000 book, *Racist America,* provides a convincing argument that "in the United States racism is structured into the rhythms of everyday life."[41] Feagin maintains that whites are privileged and blacks are disadvantaged, systematically, throughout the nation. In doing so, he provides evidence that discrimination against blacks can be found in the everyday practices of our legal, political, housing, economic, and educational systems. In fact, he notes that a recent United Nations quality-of-life index (which includes education, income, and life expectancy) ranks U.S. whites first but black Americans thirty-first, similar to residents of Trinidad and Tobago.[42]

The early twenty-first century has not revealed a brighter picture for African Americans. A 2001 Gallup poll revealed that only half of all blacks believe that they have the same job opportunities as whites and that nearly half maintain that they were discriminated against within the past month because of their race.[43] According to the U.S. Labor Department, the black unemployment rate in 2001 was still slightly more than double that of whites.

The *New York Times* series "Race in America," which won the 2000 Pulitzer Prize, provides a glimpse of the negative influence social and economic institutions in the United States can have on black-white relations. One article in the series profiled a black and a white Cuban immigrant who were best friends in Cuba.[44] Once they came to the United States, they drifted apart, one settling into the white world of Miami while the other became a member of the black Miami community. They lived, worked, and socialized in two different worlds. The white man was taught by his friends to avoid the black sections of town. The black man quickly learned firsthand that black men driving with white women in their cars can be stopped simply for "DWB" ("Driving While Black"). As the reporter, Mirta Ojito, noted, they now "inhabit a place where the color of their skin defines the outlines of their lives—where they live, the friends they make, how they speak, what they wear, even what they eat. 'It's like I am here and he is over there, [says Mr. Ruiz, who is black]. And we can't cross over to the other's world.'"

The two friends, once inseparable in Cuba, hardly ever see one another now that they live in Miami. While they previously held similar outlooks and aspirations, their worldviews and their experiences are becomingly increasingly different. They are still the same men, but their environments have changed drastically. Their friendship appears to be disintegrating because of the institutional and social separation of the white and black communities in Miami. It is also apparent that the chances are practically zero that these two men would have ever crossed the racial divide that now separates them and become friends if they had grown up in Miami.

Miami is just one example of the racial divide that exists throughout the United States. In cities, towns, and rural areas across America, blacks and whites live in largely distinct worlds. Members of both these racial groups may be Americans, but, as Andrew Hacker describes in the title to his classic book, they live in "Two Nations: Black and White, Separate, Hostile, Unequal."

Few black and white Americans interact every day as peers. As Lena Williams points out, many whites feel uncomfortable around blacks because of their inexperience with cross-racial interaction and fear that they will unintentionally appear racist. Many blacks, on the other hand, sense that whites with whom they interact view them as "examples of their race" and that they must always be on their "whitest" (i.e., most proper) behavior around whites and never let down their guard, lest they fulfill a negative stereotype whites have of blacks.

The continual rumors and urban legends about white conspiracies against blacks are stark evidence of the mistrust and suspicion that has arisen though centuries of racial oppression. Patricia Turner, in I Heard It Through the Grapevine, chronicles rumors in African American culture, from African slaves' belief that white slave dealers were cannibals to the belief of many blacks today that the U.S. government engineered the spread of AIDS among the black community (both in the United States and in Africa).[45] Even more revealing of the historic and present social separation between white and black Americans than the rumors themselves is the fact that most whites were/are completely unaware that many blacks fervently believe these conspiracy rumors. White Americans' shock that the majority of black Americans believed O.J. Simpson was innocent during his 1997 trial for murder is also indicative of the disconnect between the races.[46] When social injustices such as economic disparities, political isolation, and resentment against police shootings boil over into riots like those in New York in 1991, Los Angeles in 1992, and Cincinnati in 2001, the blacks and whites fighting each other in the streets usually have no personal connection to one another. They simply view each other as "those" people of the "other" race.

So, why then, with all these barriers, do some blacks and whites, supposed "opposites," become close friends? How do these friendships arise across the racial divide? Do you have to be colorblind to have such a friendship? Are those that do exist, to quote Benjamin DeMott, simply "masking the differences between blacks and whites"? Or can they teach us something about how blacks and whites can get along better in the United States?

The following chapters explore these questions through the words of forty pairs of close black-white friends.[47] In interviews in cities and towns across the United States, from New York to Los Angeles and from Madison to Dallas, members of black and white pairs of friends reflected on how they became friends, how they deal with the issue of race, and how their friendships have influenced their views on race and, in some cases, their actions in dealing with race in America. Unlike the popular black and white television and movie characters, all these individuals must somehow deal with the issue of race in their friendships. In sharing their stories, they provide a rare glimpse into how blacks and whites can become friends and, in doing so, cross the greatest racial divide in the United States today.

NOTES

1. Lewis Mumford Center, "Ethnic Diversity Grows, Neighborhood Integration Lags Behind," *The Lewis Mumford Center for Comparative Urban and Regional Research,* Apr. 3, Accessed at http://mumford1.dyndns.org/cen2000/report.html.

2. Sandra requested that I use her real name when quoting her. I gave all the other interviewees pseudonyms. Sandra was the only interviewee who edited her own quote. She did not, however, change any of the original content.

3. Alison Bethel, "In Living Color: The Newest Bostonians Are Multiracial, Multicultural, and Pleased to Meet You," *Boston Globe,* June 20, 1999, P30.

4. "Globe Poll: Views on Race in America," *Boston Globe Online,* May 11, 2000. Accessed at http://www.boston.com/globe/nation/packages/rethinking_integration/.

5. Marsha King, "Nibbling Away at Racial Barriers," *Seattle Times,* Jan. 16, 2000. Accessed at seattletimes.nwsource.com/news/local/html98/race20000116.html.

6. Robert W. Welkos and Richard Natale, "Multiethnic Movies Ringing True with Youths," *Los Angeles Times,* July 2, 2001. Accessed at http://www.latimes.com/news/state/20010702/t000054597.html.

7. John Fetto, "Interracial Friendships Slip?" *American Demographics* 00 (Jan. 2000). Accessed at http://www.inside.com/product/Product.asp?pfid={6A9B44F8-A949–49EE-8468-FCA343538E93}.

8. "Brown University Study: Racial biases need acknowledgment," *Masspsy.com* 9, 4 (May 2001). Accessed at http://www.masspsy.com/leading/0004_qa.html.

9. M. H. Gonzales, J. M. Davis, G. L. Loney, C. K. Kukens, and C. M. Junghans, "Interactional Approach to Interpersonal Attraction," *Journal of Personality and Social Psychology* 44 (1983): 1192–97; Theodore Newcomb, "The Prediction of Interpersonal Attraction," *American Psychologist* 11 (1956): 575–86; Newcomb, "Stabilities Underlying Changes in Interpersonal Attraction." *Journal of Abnormal and Social Psychology* 66 (1963): 376–86.

10. R. M. McWhirter and J. D. Jecker, "Attitude Similarity and Inferred Attraction," *Psychonomic Science* 7 (1967): 225–26.

11. Barney G. Glaser and Anselm Strauss, *Status Passages* (Chicago: Aldine Atherton, 1971); George J. McCall and J. L. Simmons, Identities *and Interactions* (New York: Free Press, 1978).

12. Gordon W. Allport, *The Nature of Prejudice* (New York: Doubleday, 1954); Emory S. Bogardus, *Social Distance* (Yellow Springs, OH: Antioch, 1959); William A. V. Clark, "Residential Preferences and Neighborhood Racial Segregation: A Test of the Schelling Segregation Model," *Demography* 28 (1991): 1–19.

13. William H. Tucker, *The Science and Politics of Racial Research* (Urbana: University of Illinois Press, 1994), p. 14.

14. Janes Kinney, *Amalgamation!* Westport, CT: Greenwood Press, 1985.

15. Richard Herrnstein and Charles Murray, *The Bell Curve* (New York: Free Press, 1994), is a notable exception.

16. From U.S. Department of Energy, "From the Genome to the Proteome: Basic Science" (Oak Ridge, TN: U.S. Department of Energy Office of Biological and Environmental

Research, n.d.), p. 4. For more information on the Human Genome Project, see http://www.ornl.gov/hgmis/project/info.html.

17. Mirta Ojito, "Best of Friends, Worlds Apart," *New York Times,* June 5, 2000, p. A1.

18. Vincent Parrillo, *Strangers to These Shores* (Boston: Allyn & Bacon, 2000), p. 14. Parrillo's is one of the leading textbooks in the field of race and ethnic relations today.

19. For a discussion of how the increasing number of multiracial Americans can make this common means of racial determination frustrating, see my book *From Black to Biracial* (Westport, CT: Praeger, 1999).

20. Nancy Krieger, "Counting Accountably: Implications of the New Approaches to Classifying Race/Ethnicity in the 2000 Census" American Public Health Association, 2000. Accessed at http://www.apha.org/journal/editorial/nov00/ed1nov00.htm.

21. When not otherwise noted, the information in this paragraph was derived from Natalie Angier, "Do Races Differ? Not Really, DNA Shows," *New York Times on the Web,* Aug. 22, 2000. Accessed at http://www.nytimes.com/library/national/science/082200sci-genetics-race.html.

22. Mary-Claire King, "Genomic Views of Human History," Keynote address at the HSC Poster Day, Kuwait University, April 23, 2001. Accessed at http://hscc.www.kuniv.edu.kw/poster/pages/keyspeak.htm.

23. For a useful discussion of replacing *culture* for *genes,* see Stephen Steinberg, *The Ethnic Myth* (Boston: Beacon Press, 1989).

24. See, for example, Martin Bernal, *Black Athena: The Afroasiatic Roots of Classical Civilization,* Vol. 1, *The Fabrication of Ancient Greece 1785–1985* (Newark, NJ: Rutgers University Press, 1987), and Ann Macy Roth's rejoinder, "Building Bridges to Afrocentrism," Jan. 26, 1995. Accessed at http://www.hartford-hwp.com/archives/30/134.html (originally distributed at ftp://oi.uchicago.edu/pub/papers/AMRoth_Afrocentrism.ascii.txt.)

25. Benjamin DeMott, "Put On a Happy Face: Masking the Differences Between Blacks and Whites," *Harper's Magazine,* Sept. 1995, pp. 31–38.

26. Paul Rockwell, "The Right Has a Dream: Martin Luther King as an Opponent of Affirmative Action," *Extra!,* May/June 1995. Accessed at http://www.fair.org/extra/9505/king-affirmative-action.html. See also George F. Will, "Dropping the 'One Drop' Rule," *Newsweek,* Mar. 25, 2002, p. 64.

27. Stephan Thernstrom and Abigail Thernstrom, *America in Black and White: One Nation, Indivisible* (New York: Simon & Schuster, 1997).

28. Jeff Hitchcock, *Unraveling the White Cocoon* (Dubuque, IA: Kendall/Hunt), pp. 54, 55.

29. For a more positive portrayal of biracial Americans, see my book *From Black to Biracial.*

30. See the argument of John W. Davis, Dec. 10, 1952, in *Brown et al. v. Board of Education of Topeka et al.* 347 US 483 (1954). The argument is posted at http://www.faculty.piercelaw.edu/redfield/library/Pdf/case-brown1954.pdf.

31. Over the years since the Fair Housing Act was enacted in 1968, different social scientists have carried out studies using "testers," blacks and whites given identical backgrounds and sent out to try to rent or buy the same housing. Study after study has revealed that blacks still face discrimination in the housing and rental markets. For a description of such a study see "Parsippany, New Jersey Apartment Complexes Settle Allegations of Housing Discrimination," a press release issued September 21, 2001, by

the U.S. Department of Justice on the Internet at http://www.usdoj.gov/opa/pr/2001/September/484cr.htm.

32. See, in particular, Patricia Gurin's research presented in the University of Michigan case found at http://www.umich.edu/~urel/admissions/legal/expert/gurintoc.html.

33. See Lawrence Bobo and Camille Zubrinsky, "Attitudes on Residential Integration: Perceived Status Differences, Mere In-group Preference, or Racial Prejudice?" *Social Forces* 74, 3 (1996): 883–900; Allport, *Nature of Prejudice;* Bogardus, *Social Distance;* and Cedric Herring and Charles Amissah, "Advance and Retreat: Racially Based Attitudes and Public Policy," pp. 121–43 in *Racial Attitudes in the 1990s Continuity and Change,* ed. Steven A. Tuch and Jack K. Martin (Westport, CT: Praeger, 1997).

34. Leonard Steinhorn and Barbara Diggs-Brown, *By the Color of Our Skin: The Illusion of Integration and the Reality of Race* (New York: Plume, 2000), pp. 30, 31.

35. Sarah Harris and Ron Katsuyama, Report by the Social Science Research Center at the University of Dayton for the Dayton Region of the National Conference, 1996. A description of the key results of the report can be found in a January 16, 1997, University of Dayton press release at http://www.udayton.edu/news/nr/011797.html; Christopher G. Ellison and Daniel A. Powers, "The Contact Hypothesis and Racial Attitudes Among Black Americans," *Social Science Quarterly* 75, 2 (1994): 385–400.

36. J. Blaine Hudson and Bonetta M. Hines-Hudson, "A Study of the Contemporary Racial Attitudes of Whites and African Americans," *Western Journal of Black Studies* 23, 1 (1999): 22–34.

37. Eileen O'Brien, *Whites Confront Racism: Antiracists and Their Paths to Action* (New York: Rowman & Littlefield, 2001), p. 45.

38. Lena Williams, *It's the Little Things* (New York: Harcourt, 2000), pp. 24–35.

39. DeMott, "Put On a Happy Face," pp. 31–38.

40. http://www.washingtonpost.com/wp-srv/politics/special/affirm/docs/clinton speech.htm.

41. Joe Feagin, *Racist America* (New York: Routledge, 2000), p. 2.

42. Ibid., p. 202.

43. "Differences Persist in Views of Race Relations," *Yahoo! News,* July 11, 2001. Accessed at http://dailynews.yahoo.com/htx/kgtv/20010710/lo/853917_1.html.

44. Ojito, "Best of Friends."

45. Patricia Turner, *I Heard It Through the Grapevine: Rumor in African American Culture* (Berkeley: University of California Press, 1992).

46. According to a 1997 Gallup report, 71 percent of whites believed Simpson was "probably or definitely" guilty while only 28 percent of blacks said he was "probably or definitely" guilty. See Frank Newport and Lydia Saad, "Civil Trial Didn't Alter Public's View of Simpson Case," *Gallup News Service,* Feb. 7, 1997. Accessed at http://www.gallup.com/poll/releases/pr970207.asp.

47. See Appendix A for a description of the pairs by race, age, class, and length of friendship.

2

Becoming Friends and Facing Flak

Like today, the shirt she has on is black, I had one in pink. The same one. . . . We read the same books. . . . We just have a lot in common. Like, expectations in friendships [and] expectations in relationships. Things we like to do for fun.

Jane, white, 20

There was always like one or two black kids who'd be like "What are you doing? Why are you friends with this white kid?" I'd be like "What are you talking about? Why not? I like him. He's a cool kid." And then there would come "Well, do you think you're white?"

Keith, black,[1] 21

Friendships are good for people. Those who have friends are happier, healthier, and even tend to live longer than those who live solitary lives.[2] In *Suicide*,[3] Émile Durkheim produced evidence that friendships provide people with a sense of connectedness—even a reason to live. On a societal level, friendships create connections that can bind a people together, giving them a sense of belonging and adherence to something larger than themselves.

Friendships also help us form a sense of who we are. Charles Horton Cooley, one of the founders of the symbolic interactionist perspective, said that we see ourselves as we imagine others see us. He refers to this process as the "looking glass self."[4] We create our own self-concepts based upon how we think others judge us. For instance, if I perceive that those with whom I interact view me as beautiful, I will most likely view myself as beautiful.

Symbolic interactionists also maintain that those with whom we interact frame our perspective of society. Those around us provide our immediate outlook on the world. If most people around us are suffering, we will most likely view the world as unjust. However, if the majority of people with whom we socialize are prosperous and content, we will tend to believe that our society is just. Our close friends therefore affect tremendously how we view ourselves and the world.

Friendships are unlike other primary relationships, such as those we have with siblings and parents; we develop friendships through conscious effort. No one can force us to befriend another.[5] Relations between close relatives are supported through the recognition they receive in the U.S. legal system, living arrangements, and holiday traditions. Even relatives who are estranged from one another are still related under law. Unlike siblings, who will forever be related (even if they attempt to sever communication and emotional ties with one another), friends do not need to remain friends.

Friendships can wane and even dissolve if one or the other friend loses interest. Continual effort is needed in order to maintain friendships. In her review of a book on friendships, author Megan Harlan describes the role effort plays in developing lasting adult friendships by pointing out "while faith, trust, parity and empathy all play their roles, the will to keep a friendship alive becomes, as time passes and life crowds, the relationship's most powerfully defining aspect."[6]

Friendships do not evolve through effort alone, however. Structural factors also influence with whom one is likely to become friends. Proximity and status play primary roles in friendship formation.[7] Proximity gives people the opportunity to get to know one another. Among those who interact with one another regularly, those who have the same status are most likely to become friends. Working-class people and professionals are more likely to develop friendships within their status groups than between. For instance, in a supermarket, managers and clerks may work side by side, but outside work they are most likely to socialize and become friends with people of their same status.

A popular expression about friendships, "you are who your friends are," is especially interesting when considering cross-racial friendships. Unlike the imposed relationships between siblings, friendships tend to focus on similarities. As psychologist Kory Floyd states, "unlike friends, siblings do not need to be alike to remain siblings."[8] While we are often drawn to people like ourselves, we also tend to become like those we are around. Spending time with our friends, voluntarily, leads to our beginning to identify with them to some degree.[9] Aristotle is said to have described friendship as "one soul dwelling in two bodies."[10] Because we identify with our friends, we may begin to share an outlook on society. Blacks and whites in close interracial friendships have the opportunity to see themselves and society through the eyes of someone of another race.

In order for the voluntary association that forms the basis of friendships to occur, the opportunity for interaction must exist.[11] In the 1990s, on the television show *Seinfeld*, Jerry and Kramer became friends, even though they had nothing in common, simply because they lived across the hall from one another. In time, this friendship of convenience deepened (as deep as anything can get on a show about "nothing") as they shared adventures eating at the local diner, going away on weekend trips, looking for Kramer's car in a parking garage, and so on. This show was a hit in part because we could all relate to the basic premise of what brought the characters together. All friendships form after two people's worlds somehow connect.

Close black-white friendships are no exception to this rule. The friends interviewed for this book met through work, school, church, volunteer programs, sports, or their children. Finding that they had much in common or simply enjoyed each other's company, they pursued a friendship with one another. The friends in this sample are "close" friends. They are "3:00 A.M. friends," friends who would, in case of an emergency, feel comfortable calling each other up in the middle of the night. The men and women in these friendships know each other very well, can turn to each other in times of need, and feel connected to one another. It is important to note that, in order to be included in the sample, both individuals in the friendship pairs had to describe their friendship as close and agree to an interview with the knowledge that the book focused on *close* friendships between blacks and whites.[12]

Close friendship entails mutual sharing and openness. As friends become closer, they discuss a wider range of subjects, on a deeper level, and in more relaxed and informal ways than with acquaintances or other, less close, friends.[13] Close friends are able to display a similar, thorough knowledge of the history of their friendship formation.[14] The members of the friendship pairs in this sample all told nearly identical stories of how they and their friends made the transition from acquaintances to friends to close friends.

While a small number of interviewees emphasized their differences when talking about one another, most stressed their similarities. Some shared how they were surprised to find how much they had in common with each other. Bob and Evan, two middle-class forty-something professionals who work for the same nationwide company, are a good example of friends who, at first glance, thought they were absolutely nothing like one another. They saw each other as exemplifying many of the stereotypical traits of the other race that they disliked.

Oh, we hated each other, is the way to put it. . . . Bob had a reputation of being kind of a swinging, wise, you know, black male . . . with an attitude. And I didn't like that very much. And he'll tell you he thought I was a tight ass. (Evan, white, 41)

Well, I think that Evan thought I was a typical, what he considered to be a typical, African American. That we worked off a different set of operating rules . . . and that was a barrier. . . . And I thought that he was an uptight, ultra conservative and really couldn't find the forest for the trees when it came to issues. I thought of him as being a Greek, a white Greek guy. (Bob, black, 43)

It wasn't until they were forced to work together on a project that they gradually realized that they actually had much in common. As Bob described it,

We found . . . that, once we got a chance to spend some time together, that there are certain things that we both enjoy. For instance, he likes to fish and I like to fish. He has a son and I have a son whom we hold very near and dear. . . . Our wives are both professionals. And we've had an opportunity to talk about certain things [that] come up with wives who are professionals . . . both like to travel . . . both like to run. (Bob, black, 43)

Compelled to work together by their employer, their workplace interaction helped them eventually realize that friendship potential existed between them. Their experience supports the research finding by Sias and Cahill that sharing tasks is one of the key reasons for movement from acquaintance to friend relationships among coworkers.[15] The trust that grew from their experiences at work enabled them to let their guard down with each other, discover their commonalities, and become friends so close that their colleagues refer to them as "Mutt and Jeff."

In their classic work *Identities and Interactions*, George J. McCall and J. L. Simmons wrote that "in mobile, pluralistic societies like our own . . . stereotypes attached to social identities are typically our sole source of orientation toward the majority of people we encounter. From visible clues to social identity, we connect strangers with stereotypes, so that we may predict their behavior and characteristics."[16] Whites who immediately lock their car doors when stopped in traffic in a black neighborhood or cross the street when they see a black man approach them are acting on immediate reactions based on stereotypes. Blacks who view all whites as spoiled and inconsiderate are also basing their reactions on stereotypes. Jane, an upper-middle-class college student at a southern university, spoke of how she and her black classmate Latrice had to see through first impressions in order to appreciate their similarities.

I mean like, if you were just to see me, I'm kind of like the storybook, you know, all American, blonde hair, blue eyes, pale skin. If you were to . . . like have a poster of a white person, it would probably be me. And so to then know that I love to go out and dance and like I'll go talk to anybody and . . . that I'll date black guys. Or date anybody and talk to anybody. Like a lot of people I don't think would assume that about me right off the bat. . . . Cause like when we first saw each other, you know Latrice was like "I just thought you'd be the biggest, stuck up, little, you know, just like all the other white girls at MMU." You know, and so, it's just neat how it's not like that and how much fun we do have together. Cause she's like truly one of my best friends. So . . . first impressions really aren't what you think they might be. (Jane, white, 20)

Latrice, from the lower middle class, echoed Jane's description of their underlying similarities and Aristotle's description of friendship, saying that they are "two of the same person." If they had not opened up to each other enough to learn how much they had in common, they might have retained their stereotypical notions of each other and never moved beyond the acquaintanceship level in their friendship.

Chris, a quiet black college freshman, from a primarily minority and poor city in New Jersey, was caught off his guard when a white classmate, Matt, showed signs of wanting to be his friend when they met at a training session for computer lab assistants at their university. When he was growing up,

Chris's primary connection with whites was with those he saw on television. He and his friends had stereotyped most whites as "weirdo" people.

Like [it was] already in my head . . . [to see] white people as like people who are just, you know, like real serious about like certain [things], like real serious with work. You know, they're real funny. Like they all have funny names like, you know, whatever, Tom, Bill, John. You know, like real simple names like that. And, you know, just like talking funny. Like "Hi guy." You know. [laughs] (Chris, black, 19)

Even though Chris at first thought "something was wrong" with Matt because he seemed so delighted to get to know him, they soon became inseparable. As Matt, who grew up primarily in white and middle-class suburban New Jersey, says, "A *lot* of people identify us as together. . . . I mean they *always* see us together. It's just how we are."

Chris, like Latrice, was able to recognize friendship potential, despite having a stereotyped first reaction to his white friend. Both he and Latrice were able to recognize, appreciate, and respond to their white friend's obvious interest in forming a friendship, despite the stereotypes dancing in their heads. This ability enabled Chris, Latrice, and the other interviewees, of both races, to obtain a close friend whom they now cherish.

While one pair of friends maintain that they really did become close simply because they were assigned to one another as roommates (they both say that if not forced together in that way, they never would have spent so much time with someone so different from themselves), the vast majority found they had much in common. Many quickly realized that they had many similarities. In these friendships, the racial divisiveness common among many blacks and whites, and noted in the prevailing literature on friendship formation, appears not to exist. For instance, Rod and Vinnie, childhood friends who played sports together as working-class scholarship students at the same prep school in a large northeastern city, now teach and coach football together at another prep school in New England. Rod referred to them as

A pretty dynamic duo, I think. But I think that it's all based on our initial friendship. I mean we were both scholarship kids at St. Andrews's. . . . And, of course, the other camaraderie [we] have is from the field. . . . It bonded us. . . . I was a back and he was a lineman. So, he blocked for me. Well, it hasn't changed. It's never changed. I look out for him and he opens doors for me. . . . No matter what roads we've taken . . . we always keep coming back to the original camaraderie. And nothing gets between it. And around here, everyone knows. Like, you can say anything, you can do whatever you want, but no one, no one can cross our friendship. Because that's, that's like the highest thing. So, whenever someone does do anything to me or him, then they got both of us. (Rod, 45, black)

Rod and Vinnie are known all across the campus for their mutual love of sports and their loyalty and devotion to one another.

Carol and Tracy, two middle-class professional women who met in the seminary, also believe that commonalities sparked their friendship. Carol describes
how they became friends:

We had a lot in common. She was attending a church like the church I had attended
. . . which was very much opposed to the ordination of women. And so we had that
experience in common. Cause most . . . of the [other] women who came to the seminary
came from parishes that were in favor of the ordination of women. And so they didn't
even think about, you know, these communities where women's ministry was not affirmed. And so Tracy and I both had that experience of being from parishes where most
of the people were against the ordination of women. And Tracy is a singer, and I'm a
singer. And Tracy's an actress. And I wouldn't call myself an actress, but I have been in
plays and I've been in operas and stuff. (Carol, 50, black)

Tracy and Carol's friendship sprang, in part, from their uniting as part of a
small number of women seminarians from patriarchal church backgrounds.
However, beyond the political/religious connections, they enjoy each other's
company simply because they share many talents, personality traits, and interests.

Two other interviewees, Elaine and Kathy, now in their twenties, bonded as
the only thirteen-year-olds chosen for parts in one of their local midwestern
university's theater productions. Spending rehearsals laughing and giggling
together, they realized they had both theatrical and athletic interests in common. Their experience with the university theater spawned a friendship that
has lasted almost two decades.

Paul and Keith became close friends in their New England college. While
Keith initially thought that Paul was "the biggest asshole he ever met," the
two gradually recognized that they had much in common underneath the first,
surface, impressions they had of one another. While Paul came from the high
end and Keith grew up in the lower end of the middle class, they both are
bright, enjoy working together to promote various causes around campus, and
share a sharp and rather caustic sense of humor. Paul was almost at a loss for
words when he tried to describe the bond between himself and Keith.

It's hard to describe why we're such good friends, other than we really get along on
every level that there is to talk about, you know. And it's funny because my other two
best friends were best friends from childhood . . . they were both white. I knew them,
and, through[out the years], when we were little kids, we did everything together. And
I would say that in the span of two years or three years, Keith has reached that level if
not surpassed it as being, you know . . . one of my two best friends. And I can't really
describe why, it's kind of strange. (Paul, white, 22)

Paul and Keith connect so well, they plan on traveling across Europe and the
United States together before they both go to graduate school on the West
Coast.

The stories of these friendships are not those of opposites attracting. If nothing else, they have in common what initially brought them together. However, as noted in chapter 1, many black and white Americans never interact as peers. Many see each other, as Chris put it, only on television. They miss even the opportunity to become friends. When physical proximity does exist, cultural segregation can work to reduce interaction. Cultural assumptions of difference and mistrust are barriers to contact even when blacks and whites share the same physical space.

WHITE RESISTANCE TO CLOSE
BLACK-WHITE FRIENDSHIPS

In some ways, it appears that whites are much more open to interracial friendships than blacks. Whites who establish friendships with blacks are not usually criticized by other whites for doing so. (It is important to remember that these friendships are all platonic. Whites' reactions to interracial dating and marriage are far more negative than they are to interracial friendships.)[17] In fact, many white interviewees describe reactions by fellow whites such as "Oh, you have a black friend. How nice!" The implication is that their friendships are either a nice novelty or a sign that there are no problems between blacks and whites in the United States.

However, a white person's portrayal of a pair of close black-white friends as evidence of good relations and equality between the races ignores the reality that it is the discrimination wrought by white America against black Americans that has made friendship opportunities between the races so rare. In *American Apartheid*, Douglas Massey and Nancy Denton make a convincing case that white personal and institutional discrimination against blacks has created a dramatic residential separation between the races. David James expands upon Massey and Denton's argument and notes that "racial segregation [acts to] reinforce racial attitudes and prejudices."[18] Purposive discrimination by white Americans has created a nation in which blacks and whites live in isolation from one another and see one another primarily through stereotypes fostered by the media and hearsay rather than direct, personal interaction.

Leonard Steinhorn declares that Martin Luther King's vision of integration "remains for most blacks a far-off distant dream."[19] He maintains that whites still do not want to live around blacks. White resistance to living in proximity to blacks remains even when controlling for socio-economic status. While the process is subtler than the white flight of decades past, when even affluent blacks begin to move into a white neighborhood, whites start to move out. Supposedly integrated neighborhoods are frequently in transition from white to black.

As described in chapter 1, evidence of the continual pervasiveness of racism in areas of society outside residential arrangements also abounds. As Joe Feagin noted in his study of middle-class black Americans in the late 1980s and early

1990s, blacks of all social classes must deal with antiblack discrimination.[20] News reports reveal that Feagin's work over a decade ago still holds true. In 1999 the state of New Jersey publicly admitted that its state troopers had carried out racial profiling for years.[21] Coca-Cola[22] and the Adam's Mark[23] hotel chain settled major racial discrimination lawsuits in 2000. In 2001 news reports indicated that Nissan Motor Company's finance policies for automobile buyers discriminate against African Americans.[24] According to the Southern Poverty Law Center, incidents of racial hatred occur with increasing frequency on our college campuses.[25] Most of the blacks interviewed for this book reported facing derogatory epithets and other forms of racial discrimination throughout their lives. The fact is that these friendships have developed *in spite of* historical and present discrimination against blacks.

BLACK RESISTANCE TO CLOSE
BLACK-WHITE FRIENDSHIPS

Most of the young black men and women who do meet and become close friends with whites have to deal with criticism from members of their own race for doing so. Ninety percent of the black interviewees under thirty described facing disapproval of their cross-racial friendships from black friends, family, or acquaintances. As illustrated above, this reaction is different from the responses whites in such friendships receive from other whites. Whites do not have the same sense of racial group salience that blacks have. With few having faced discrimination based on their race, whites do not identify themselves as part of an oppressed group whose members must stay united for support and protection.[26] Unlike whites, who have little reason to feel threatened when one of their group befriends a black person, many blacks resent when one of "their own" chooses to associate closely with whites. When a fellow black becomes close friends with a member of the racial group in society that has traditionally oppressed and often worked to divide them, many view it as consorting with the enemy.[27]

While middle-class blacks growing up in predominantly white suburban neighborhoods might not have a choice of races to associate with, the sense of group solidarity among blacks remains generally strong, despite class differences.[28] Many blacks now in the middle class were born into poor families and are reminded often of their ties to other blacks across class lines when they get together with family members who still live in poor, racially isolated neighborhoods.[29] These ties are further cemented when they face incidents of racial discrimination.

Given the fact that few black families are more than a generation away from racial isolation and poverty and none are immune from racial discrimination, it makes sense that some might view other blacks associating with whites with suspicion. As Kobe, a young man from a predominantly poor black city in New Jersey surmises,

I guess in Brockville, you don't see many white people there. Everybody has their own sort of image of who you should hang with and who you shouldn't hang with. (Kobe, black, 28)

While Kobe has broken out of this pattern of excluding white people and become close platonic friends with a white woman, he clearly recognizes that he has broken a "rule" in doing so. The majority of the stories black interviewees shared of facing disapproval of their friendships with whites involved poor blacks directing negative remarks to middle-class blacks. Like those in Kobe's neighborhood, these blacks from poorer economic backgrounds tend to regard whites as a monolithic "other" that they look at with more fear and resentment than thoughts of potential friendships.

High school and college can be an especially trying time for blacks who cross the racial divide. During this period of development, many adolescent and young adult blacks start to build a strong sense of a black racial identity. All children begin to establish an understanding of who they are when they enter adolescence. Black teenagers in a race-based society are constantly reminded that they are black and living in a society where whiteness is viewed as superior to blackness.

William Cross describes five stages of black racial identity development (preencounter, encounter, immersion/emersion, internalization, and internalization-commitment) in *Shades of Black*.[30] According to Cross, during the preencounter stage, the black person has internalized the dominant racial ideology in the United States and believes that it is better to be white than black. Entrance into the encounter stage is precipitated by a firsthand experience of the negative effects of racism. Blacks begin to be aware of and to wrestle with the fact that they are black in a white-dominated society. Those who enter the immersion/emersion stage deal with this knowledge by surrounding themselves with symbols of blackness and with fellow blacks. Their hurt at being the victim of racism is transformed into feelings of black pride and white avoidance. Those who leave this stage and enter the internalization stage have gained a sense of what it means to be black, feel comfortable with their black identity, and are ready to deal with members of other races. Blacks who reach the internalization-commitment stage are capable of forming coalitions with members of other racial groups in efforts to fight racism.

Attempting to find a positive identity and yet facing the realization of racial discrimination in U.S. society, many young blacks enter the immersion/emersion stage in high school. During this period of their lives, many undergo what Cross describes as the "'Blacker-than-thou' syndrome . . . passing judgment on whether or not a person has the 'appropriate' level of Blackness."[31] Those in this stage neither appreciate nor understand why a black person would want to have white friends.[32]

Beverly Daniel Tatum describes Cross's stages of racial identity in her aptly titled book "*Why Are All the Black Kids Sitting Together in the Cafeteria?*"[33]

She points out that these stages are not necessarily confined to certain periods in a lifetime. People can maintain, ascend, or descend stages throughout their lives.

However, it is worth noting that the black interviewees over the age of thirty either did not describe any criticism from other blacks about their cross-racial friendships or said that they had not received any "since grade school." It is important to recognize that these interviewees are not in peer-pressure-dominated environments where identity formation is one's primary work, like high school and college, with which the younger interviewees must cope. They are also more likely than younger blacks to have already passed through the Blacker-than-thou stage of racial identity that William Cross describes. Finally, the older interviewees also grew up before the black power movement and the popularization of black separatism in the late 1960s and early 1970s and, therefore, are less influenced by that mode of thought than the younger interviewees.

Blacks who are at other stages of black racial identity development than the "Blacker-than-thou stage, such as those interviewed, do not have a general antipathy toward whites. Two-thirds of the blacks in the friendship pairs now in college were raised on the white side of the divide and grew up, predominantly, around white people in middle-class suburban neighborhoods. While they may share opinions with poor blacks on the government's obligation to curb racial discrimination in U.S. society, they are accustomed to dealing with and relating to whites. The main concern for most of these younger interviewees is not discrimination from whites but antipathy from other blacks. They neither understand nor appreciate being told by other blacks that friendship with whites is somehow a sign of a lack of "true" blackness.

Keith, raised in a relatively racially and economically diverse section of a major city in Pennsylvania, was one of many young interviewees who expressed exasperation and puzzlement at the criticism he received for socializing with whites. At the summer camp he attended as a child, Keith faced some negative comments from black campers when he became friends with some of the white campers.

There was always like one or two black kids who'd be like, "What are you doing? Why are you friends with this white kid?" I'd be like "What are you talking about? Why not? I like him. He's a cool kid." And then there would come, "Well, do you think you're white?" (Keith, black, 21)

Even the preteen boys at Keith's camp understood the implicit rule that blacks and whites should not be friends.

The few black interviewees who feel more comfortable around whites than blacks had an especially difficult time. Steven faced the disapproval of his black peers when he associated primarily with whites in high school.

I don't wear the same kinds of clothes, you know, as the stereotype of black people would. And so, I think in high school, where, you know, a lot of people are kind of small-minded about things, you know, they would see somebody like me and they would immediately go to the "Well, why is he so trying to be white?" or "trying to fit into that group?" But it's not that I was just trying to fit into that group, it was just, that was me. That was what I came up to be. And, you know, I've always dressed the way I dress and spoke the way I've spoken. So, it's never been an issue for me but, you know, I have had those dirty stares in the hall. (Steven, black, 19)

Steven makes the point here that he wasn't trying to "act white." He was simply being himself. Raised in a white, middle-class, suburban neighborhood in the South by his mother, who chose to move there for the good schools, Steven shares most of the cultural traits of his fellow middle-class suburban classmates, who happen to be white. The black kids at school who gave him "dirty stares in the hall" were bused in from the predominantly poor and black inner city. One of the few things Steven and they had in common was the color of their skin. That was not enough to make them feel connected to one another.

Steven's middle-class status and his proximity to white, middle-class peers in both his school and his neighborhood have made him culturally, in many ways, more similar to his white than his black classmates. In addition to his taste in clothes and manner of speech, the activities that Steven was interested in were also popular among the white children with whom he grew up.

I did choir and theater and things like that. And those aren't—I don't know—I guess they weren't things that interested black people of my high school. So the activities and the friends that I already had just kind of carried on in the high school. And so, you know [slight laugh], it's carried me through college, too. (Steven, black, 19)

Steven's upbringing, in effect, was very similar to those of his white neighbors and classmates but not at all like the poor inner-city blacks bused into his high school or like the blacks he has, so far, encountered in college.

On the other hand, Steven's mother, like many other first-generation middle-class blacks, has retained ties to the black community where she grew up. All her close friends are black. She, like Steven's urban classmates, has had some difficulty with Steven's becoming so comfortable in his white middle-class surroundings.

Steven's mother was one of the few parents, of either the white or the black interviewees, who had strong reservations about the cross-racial friendships their children made. In the few cases of interviewees' black parents expressing such concerns, their stated motive was to ensure that their children remembered their black roots. Like most middle-class blacks, the vast majority of the black interviewees, even if in the middle or upper middle class today, have not-too-distant family connections to the lower socioeconomic classes. In most cases, black roots implies a class (lower) as well as a racial and cultural status. This puts black interviewees who grew up in middle-class, predominantly white, neighborhoods into a double bind. There are few, if any, middle-class blacks around with whom to socialize. Moreover, the blacks they do meet at school tend to be bused in from poorer neighborhoods. While their parents may have a similar economic background as their children's classmates, the middle-class black interviewees themselves tend to have little in common with them. They belong to the same race but their different economic statuses and outlooks for the future often impede the development of friendships between them.

Ese, a black undergraduate on a predominantly white university campus in the South, talked about how painful it was to feel shunned by both white and black students for trying to participate in a rush for traditionally white sororities. While her best friend in high school was black, she, like Steven, grew up predominantly around whites and felt more comfortable around whites than around blacks. Indeed, she always pictured herself as being a member of a mostly white sorority when she went to college. She thought of herself as a "typical" sorority girl. She was not at all prepared for the reception she received from both the white and the black students on campus.

Well, out of 550 girls, I was the only black girl rushing. And at this point, it did make me feel uncomfortable because, like, you had to wear these name badges and everywhere that I'd walk, other black kids would be like "Do you know what rush you're going through?" I'd go meet a group of black girls and they'd be like, "Oh, you're that girl." It's like everyone was talking about me and I was just like . . . that black girl that's going through rush. The wrong rush. (Ese, black, 21)

Although she was her high school class president and had very high grades, good looks, and perfect "party scores" in all the houses she visited, Ese was not accepted by any of the sorority houses on campus. She found out later that some sororities had house meetings during which they decided not to invite her. One sorority president said at her sorority's meeting that they had already fulfilled their minority "quota." (The one Hispanic woman in that house resigned in protest, saying she did not want to be anyone's "quota.")

After the rush debacle, Ese felt isolated from both whites and blacks on campus.

So, yah, I was really hurt because . . . I felt like I wasn't accepted by the white people on campus . . . in my first, like, four weeks here. And then, of course, the black kids were just like, they didn't want to talk to me cause they're like, you know "There's that girl who went through that rush." (Ese, black, 21)

Her friendship with her best friend Peggy, a white middle-class student across the hall who was bright and very sociable but not interested in joining a sorority, helped Ese get through the difficult beginning to her college career. Seeing each other constantly in the dorm, the two became very close friends.

I'd run across the hall. I'd always sleep on her floor or in [her roommate's] bed. And then ah, I don't know. We just. We started. We both joined . . . a Christian . . . [organization] here. . . . That's probably where we met. . . . And we just did a lot together after that. . . . She wasn't in any sorority, I wasn't in any sorority and we'd go eat together, dinner, every night. And we just had a blast, you know. (Ese, black, 21)

Her friendship with Peggy helped assuage some of her hurt feelings and focus her energies elsewhere. However, three years later, Ese still feels the pain and shock of the rejection from so many of her white and black classmates.

The most common criticism that young black interviewees faced from other blacks concerned their manner of speech. Language, an integral part of culture, tends to vary in form and style between poor blacks who live in isolation from whites and middle-class blacks who live among many whites. As noted earlier, two-thirds of the interviewees under thirty grew up in predominantly white middle-class environments. These interviewees spoke repeatedly of receiving negative remarks for speaking "white." As Joe Feagin has pointed out "being middle-class often means that you, as many blacks say, 'sound white.'"[35] Latrice, who grew up in a primarily white neighborhood in the South, described such comments:

And I *always* got flak about how proper I speak. . . . Black people were always like, "Why do you talk like that?" [laughs] And I'm like "Like what? This is standard English. What do you mean?" [laughs] So, I always got flak about that. Always. (Latrice, black, 19)

Speaking "proper" meant speaking "white." Ese says she constantly hears the phrase "You talk like a white girl."

You know, I hear that all the time, like, when I . . . would go out . . . to like, more, predominantly black neighborhoods. . . . [And at college] I'd find myself not talking around certain black people because I did not want to get made fun of. (Ese, black, 21)

A naturally talkative, gregarious young woman, Ese felt that she could not be herself around some black people for fear of being ridiculed.

James, another young black interviewee, who was raised in a primarily white neighborhood in New Jersey, went so far as to actually change the way he spoke in order to fit in better with his black high school friends. While in advanced classes with predominantly white classmates, James's closest friends were the black kids with whom he played sports.

My friends [in high school] used to always make fun of me about [the way I would] speak. . . . They would always like critique me on how I spoke. So, somewhere between my junior and senior year, I was just like, okay. And this was a stupid thing I did. I just stopped speaking like that and just spoke more like them . . . toward their standards. . . . And now I can't even speak the way I used to. I guess it just made it easier for us to associate and stuff. Cause they were my close friends [and closer] than the few [white] friends I had in my classes. (James, black, 18)

While he regrets the change now, James felt compelled to alter a part of himself, namely his manner of speech, in order to feel accepted by his black friends in high school. Not feeling close to the majority of his white classmates, James was willing to give up something of himself in order to feel accepted by his black friends. All the interviewees who faced this pressure to conform, to somehow blend themselves into what their black peers declared to be appropriate cultural behavior, fought a constant battle to justify various aspects of their lives, including their friendships with white people.

CULTURE AND RACE

Mary Waters points out, in *Black Identities: West Indian Immigrant Dreams and American Realities*,[36] that most whites do not recognize the ethnic heterogeneity among black Americans. However, black immigrants vary in cultural background with their nation of origin, and immigrants as a group differ significantly in their outlooks and experiences from African Americans. This research reveals the generally overlooked cultural variations that also exist among African Americans. Class background strongly influences the values and beliefs of all Americans. Just as working-class whites view society differently from upper-class whites, poor and middle-class African Americans also have different perspectives and outlooks.

Culturally, the black interviewees fall into a plethora of the various subcultures within the United States. Their cultural backgrounds vary according to the types of people with whom they have interacted most often. Most are bicultural, feeling relatively comfortable in both black and white settings. Some, like Kobe, are most comfortable in a relatively poor working-class African American culture. Ese, whose father is from Nigeria, feels most at home in either an upper-middle-class white or a Nigerian American environment. Steven, on the other hand, is most at ease around middle-class whites.

The interviewees also vary in how many white friends they have. Kobe, like the majority of the other lower- and working-class black interviewees, has only one close white friend. All Steven's close friends are white. Latrice, from the lower middle class, has a mixture of white and black close friends.

However, no matter what their culture or how many white friends they may have, racially all the black interviewees are black.[37] Each acknowledges that the average person passing them on the street views them as black. Therefore, they must all deal with the racism that pervades U.S. society. These men and women are aware that, even if they socialize solely with whites and speak only "proper" English, they will remain black in a society that increasingly defines race on the basis of appearance.[38] They are not confused about their race and they resent any implication that they might be.

Kia, a young black woman from a predominantly white suburb in the South, who has many close white friends, says that she has a very clear and strong sense of her own racial identity.

I've encountered a lot of comments like, you know, "Kia doesn't even know she's black." . . . It just always was so amusing to me how much these people didn't know me. And that was the comfort of it. Because they didn't know me. So, obviously, if you knew me, you wouldn't make a comment such as that. . . . I think it's awesome [to have close white friends]. And I see it as a blessing and a learning experience. And it's just done so much for me. And I just think the most important part, and I love my parents for [being] able to instill this in me without me forgetting who I am. You know, like . . . I can, for instance, you know, spout off black history. I can . . . tell you what it means to me to be an African American. [I can] fight against discrimination, probably be on Oprah one day, whatever, whatever. But still have those friendships, you know. And [I'm] to the point where I know what's right and I know what's wrong. And I know who I am. And I'm not giving in and I'm not, you know, like assimilating or whatever. But I'm making the essence of my true self, you know, mix with others. So, [I'm] being myself and this is still happening. [I'm] not having to, you know, conform to being quote unquote white to have these friendships. (Kia, black, 18)

Kia is both proud of being black and thankful for having the opportunity to have close white friends. She sees no contradiction between the two.

However, as Kia suggests, African Americans and white Americans have had very different histories in the United States. Whites have not had to see themselves as a cohesive race. Ruth Frankenberg points out in *White Women, Race Matters: The Social Construction of Whiteness* that cultural identity and power are inversely related. Groups that are furthest from the center of power are more often perceived as possessing a distinct and readily identifiable culture than those closest to the center. Whites tend not to notice their own culture. Instead, they normalize it and use it, unconsciously, to mark those who differ from it. As Frankenberg puts it, "whiteness comes to be an unmarked or neutral category, whereas other cultures are specifically marked 'cultural.' . . . Whites are the nondefined definers of other people."[39]

Like Tabitha, a nineteen-year-old white interviewee from a primarily white suburb in New Jersey, most whites do not believe they have a particular culture.

The only time I was ever really like wow, Maria's *black* is like she almost joined like um, like a racial sorority on campus. And, for some reason like, it just was like Oh! Hmm! Because, it's like a multiracial like sorority. If I wanted to join I could. But on the other hand, like, it was like, it was kind of like about culture and stuff. It was like, I don't really have one. [laughs] Like, the white people. Like, as a white person, do you feel like you have culture, you know. [laughs] Like I don't. [laughs] I don't. And, I don't know. For some reason, I was like wow! It didn't bother me. I was like that's kind of cool. [laughs] Like I don't have any to give. [laughs] (Tabitha, white, 19)

Tabitha does not believe she, as a white person, has any culture to contribute to a multicultural sorority. In this statement, she illustrates Frankenberg's argument that whites assign distinct cultures to minority groups but perceive themselves as simply normal and without culture.

Echoing Frankenberg, George Lipsitz writes in *The Possessive Investment in Whiteness*, "as the unmarked category against which difference is constructed, whiteness never has to speak its name, never has to acknowledge its role as an organizing principle in social and cultural relations."[40] While unacknowledged, race has benefited white Americans throughout the history of the United States. As Lipsitz describes in detail, white Americans, as a group, have worked unceasingly to elevate their status at the expense of racial minorities, all the while blaming the inferior position of minorities on their genes or culture.

The people who make up these pairs of friends are not of the same race, and race still matters. While in very different ways, the perspectives of both the white and the black friends are affected by race. Every American sees the world through race-tinted lenses.

The majority of these friends were drawn to one another because of their commonalities. This fact indicates that social scientists' understanding of homophily must be updated to include the possibility of "like attracting like" across the racial divide. However, that does not mean that race does not play a role in these friendships. Whether black or white, all these friends have to deal with the reality that their close friends are of a race that has traditionally been portrayed as unlike, even "opposite," their own. Interracial friendships take place in a society in which race affects everything—including friendships. Chapter 3 reveals the various ways that cross-racial friends deal with the issue of race in their friendships.

NOTES

1. Keith has a white mother and a black father but says he is perceived as black.

2. Judy Turner, Miroslava Lhotsky, and Peggy Edwards, *The Healthy Boomer* (Toronto: McClelland & Steward/Tundra Books, 2000); Jenny Gravacs, "Your Health." *Industry Week* 245, 18 (Oct. 7, 1996): 94; Darcy Clay Siebert, Elizabeth J. Mutran, and Donald C. Reitzes, "Friendship and Social Support: The Importance of Role Identity to Aging Adults," *Social Work* 44, 6 (1999): 522–33.

3. Émile Durkheim, *Suicide* (New York: Free Press, 1997).

4. Charles Horton Cooley, *Human Nature and the Social Order* (New York: Schocken Books, 1902).

5. See W. K. Rawlins, *Friendship Matters: Communication, Dialectics, and the Life Course* (New York: Aldine de Gruyter, 1992), esp. p. 9.

6. Megan Harlan, "Review of *Into the Tangle of Friendship*, by Beth Kephart," *New York Times Book Review*, Oct. 1, 2000, p. 18.

7. James Wiggins, Beverly Wiggins, and James Vander Zanden, *Social Psychology* (New York: McGraw-Hill, 1994), pp. 354–55.

8. Floyd Kory, "Gender and Closeness Among Friends and Siblings," *Journal of Psychology* 129, 2 (1995): 193–202.

9. Wiggins, Wiggins, and Vander Zanden, *Social Psychology*.

10. Diogenes Laertius, *Lives of the Philosophers* (Cambridge: Harvard University Press). Vol. 5, p. 25, 1969).

11. E. Griffin and G. G. Sparks, "Friends Forever: A Longitudinal Exploration of Intimacy in Same-Sex Pairs and Platonic Pairs," *Journal of Social and Personal Relationships* 7 (1990): 29–46; L. Nahemow and M. P. Lawton, "Similarity and Propinquity in Friendship Formation," *Journal of Personality and Social Psychology* 32 (1975): 205–

13; Patricia Sias and Daniel J. Cahill, "From Coworkers to Friends: The Development of Peer Friendships in the Workplace," *Western Journal of Communication* 62, 3 (1998): 273–99.

12. I had to replace only one of the pairs for lack of "closeness" in the relationship. When asked about the strength of the friendship during the interview, one of the friends said the two were friends but not "close" friends.

13. I. Altman and D. A. Taylor, *Social Penetration: The Development of Interpersonal Relationships* (New York: Holt, Rinehart and Winston, 1973); M. L. Knapp, *Social Intercourse: From Greeting to Goodbye* (Boston: Allyn & Bacon, 1978); D. Jerome, "Good Company: The Sociological Implications of Friendship," *Sociological Review* 32 (1984): 696–715; S. Planalp, and A. Benson, "Friends' and Acquaintances' Conversations I: Perceived Differences," *Journal of Social and Personal Relationships* 9 (1992): 483–506.

14. Sias and Cahill, "From Coworkers to Friends."

15. Ibid.

16. George J. McCall and J. L. Simmons, *Identities and Interactions* (New York: Free Press, 1978).

17. According to a 1997 Gallup Poll, 61 percent of whites compared to 77 percent of blacks approve of interracial marriages. Charlotte Astor, "Gallup Poll: Progress in Black/White Relations, but Race Is Still an Issue," *USIA Electronic Journal* 2, 3 (Aug. 1997). Accessed at http://usinfo.state.gov/journals/itsv/0897/ijse/gallup.htm. While this was not a question examined for this book, only a slightly higher percentage of white and black interviewees expressed approval of interracial romantic relationships. I was surprised that a significant minority of those with close cross-racial friends disapprove of interracial dating and marriage.

18. Douglas S. Massey and Nancy A. Denton, "The Construction of the Ghetto," pp. 178–201; and David R. James, "The Racial Ghetto as a Race Making Situation," pp. 400–416; both in *Majority and Minority: The Dynamics of Race and Ethnicity in American Life*, ed. Norman R. Yetman (Boston: Allyn & Bacon, 1999).

19. Leonard Steinhorn, "Martin Luther King's Half-Won Battle," *Ace Magazine*, Feb. 2000. Accessed at http://www.aceweekly.com/acemag/backissues/000202/cb000202.html.

20. Joe R. Feagin, "The Continuing Significance of Race: Antiblack Discrimination in Public Places," *American Sociological Review* 56 (1991): 101–16.

21. Amy Worden, "Federal Probe Ends in Racial Profiling Pact,'" *APBnews.com*, Jan. 14, 2000. Accessed at http://www.apbnews.com/cjprofessionals/behindthebadge/2000/01/14/racial0114_01.html?s = emil.ner.

22. Kimberly Hohman, "Coke Settles Discrimination Suit," *About.com*, Nov. 2000. Accessed at http://racerelations.about.com/newsissues/racerelations/library/weekly/aa112000a.htm.

23. Katie Hooten, "Hotel Chain to Pay $8 Million to Settle Racial Bias Lawsuits," The Meeting Professional International, March 2000. 7, 13. Accessed at http://www.mpiweb.org/default.asp.

24. Linda Bean, "Shopping For Credit: Nissan Case Spawns Tips for Consumers," *DiversityInc.com*, July 9, 2001. Accessed at http://www.diversityinc.com/public/1166.cfm.

25. Southern Poverty Law Center, "Hate Goes to School," *Intelligence Report*, Spring 2000. Accessed at http://www.splcenter.org/cgi-bin/goframe.pl?refname = /intelligence project/ip-arch.html.

26. Ashley W. Doane Jr., "Dominant Group Ethnic Identity in the United States," *Sociological Quarterly* 38, 3 (Summer 1997): 375–97.

27. In the plantation past, blacks were divided between field hands and house slaves. Today, many whites divide those black persons they label "black" (middle-class blacks with whom whites interact in primarily white settings) from those they associate with the epithet "nigger" (those they associate with poverty, crime, and welfare).

28. T. Bledsoe, S. Welch, L. Sigelman, and M. Combs, "Suburbanization, Residential Integration, and Racial Solidarity Among African Americans," Paper presented at the annual meeting of the Midwest Political Science Association, Chicago, April 1994; Steven A. Tuch, Lee Sigelman, and Jack K. Martin, "Fifty Years After Myrdal: Blacks' Racial Policy Attitudes in the 1990s," pp. 226–38 in *Racial Attitudes in the 1990s*, ed. Steven A. Tuch and Jack K. Martin (Westport, CT: Praeger, 1997).

29. Bart Landry, *The New Black Middle Class* (Berkeley: University of California Press, 1987). Middle-class blacks are often raised in "buffer neighborhoods" between poor blacks and middle-class whites. See Mary Pattillo-McCoy, *Black Picket Fences: Privilege and Peril Among the Black Middle Class* (Chicago: University of Chicago Press, 1999).

30. William E. Cross Jr., *Shades of Black: Diversity in African-American Identity* (Philadelphia: Temple University Press, 1999).

31. Ibid., p. 205.

32. Beverly Daniel Tatum, *"Why Are All the Black Kids Sitting Together in the Cafeteria?"* (New York: Basic Books, 1997).

33. Ibid.

34. Keith has a white mother and a black father but says he is perceived as black.

35. Feagin, "Continuing Significance," 110.

36. Mary C. Waters, *Black Identities: West Indian Immigrant Dreams and American Realities* (Cambridge, MA: Harvard University Press, 1999).

37. Two are actually biracial (white-black and Asian-black) but say that they are perceived as black.

38. See Kathleen Korgen and Jeffry Korgen, "From the 'One Drop Rule' to the Pigmentation Rule," *Southeastern Sociological Review* 1 (2000): 1–14.

39. Ruth Frankenberg, *White Women, Race Matters: The Social Construction of Whiteness* (Minneapolis: University of Minnesota Press, 1993).

40. George Lipsitz, *The Possessive Investment in Whiteness* (Philadelphia: Temple University Press, 1998).

3

The Elephant in the Living Room

I can't even think of any one thing that we've talked about in terms of race. Because it's just—you know, we're friends. That's where it is. That's the way it is.

Kofi, black, 35

[Race does not come up] at all. Except for when we're like, ripping on each other.

Paul, white, 18

I think race died down a long time ago in Vinnie's and my relationship. Now, it's personal [laughs]. It's just personal. . . . It just doesn't come up anymore except when talking about others and their deal with race.

Rod, black, 45

There is no escaping the fact that we live in a race-conscious and divided society. All blacks and whites in close interracial friendships must somehow deal with this reality of race as they interact with their close friends. Consciously or not, the pair must agree upon and carry out a strategy to somehow "demilitarize" the topic of race and discuss it with defenses down or somehow find a way to sidestep the subject while still remaining close to one another.

Some friends used their racial differences to learn from one another, but most acted as if the differences did not exist. In either case, the friends actively constructed a means to "disarm" the topic, so that it would not come between them and harm their friendships. Each pair developed its own means of handling the delicate task. However, it is possible to discern three primary behavioral patterns by which the forty pairs of friends in this sample dealt with the issue of race in their relationships:

Ignoring/avoiding the topic of race

Joking about race

Seriously discussing racial issues

While some pairs exhibited traits from more than one category, one of the three strategies was clearly dominant in each of the dyads.

IGNORING/AVOIDING RACE

Just as race does not play a major role in the development of cross-racial friendships, it is not usually a topic of serious discussion in most close black-white friendships. As Walid Affifi and Laura Guerrero suggest, in their article "Some Things Are Better Left Unsaid II: Topic Avoidance in Friendships,"[1] the discussion of racial issues in cross-racial friendships is not necessarily an indication of the closeness of these relationships. Topic avoidance is not uncommon in close friendships. While self-disclosure is an integral part of such relationships,[2] researchers also now note that people consider some topics to be taboo and avoid discussing them even with close friends.[3]

As in platonic cross-sex close friendships in which dating and sexual experiences are rarely discussed,[4] many close interracial friends do not talk to one another about racial issues. Affifi and Guerrero maintain that individuals in cross-sex friendships avoid discussing such topics as dating and sex at the "heart" of the tension in many such relationships. Friends in platonic cross-sex relationships deal with what communication scholars Samter and Cupach describe as "the need to 'de-emphasize' sexuality."[5] The majority of these interracial friends deal with their racial differences by avoiding or ignoring the issue of race in their relationships. Whether consciously or not, the majority of these pairs have managed to avoid the volatile topic of race just as platonic cross-sex friends stay away from the issue of sex.

Twenty of the forty pairs rarely discuss the issue of race. While there is no overt attempt to ignore or sidestep the topic, it seldom arises. When race does become a focus of conversation, the discussion usually consists of

discussions of what seem, at least to the white friend, seemingly isolated experiences of discrimination the black friend has faced

brief debates about unavoidable, national, race-related incidents (e.g., O.J. Simpson's guilt or innocence)

the topic of "light" conversation (e.g., importance of considering skin tones when purchasing clothes and makeup)

Kyle and Patrick provide a good example of avoiding the issue of race. As Kyle, a white middle-class college student from a primarily white suburb in the Northeast, puts it, race is "never" something that "enters into our relationship."

It's not even like something that comes up in like conversation. Even now, it's like me and him, and just, and all my friends and stuff. We just, you know, Pat is Pat. We don't look at him as being black or whoever, you know. I never. I mean, obviously we know he is. But it just never, it never like enters into our relationship. (Kyle, white, 23)

One of the few times that Kyle remembers discussing race occurred when he, with Pat and some white friends, was pulled over by the police in a car.

They'd [the police] pull him over and they, you know, they pulled me and my friends and he'd be in the car and they'd think we'd be up to you know. . . . [We'd] say it's ridiculous. [We'd] say and Pat would say "the reason they're doing this and that, you know, [is] because I'm black." It's a typical, you know, stereotype that if you're black, you're some kind of criminal. You know, and I know he's encountered that, stuff like that. And it offends him, you know, it's ridiculous. It offends, you know, it offends me, it offends my friends. (Kyle, white, 23)

Those conversations, though, did not occur either outside such incidents or discussions of current news events.

Paula, a white middle-class graduate student raised in a predominantly white immigrant urban community, also remembers that one of the rare times she and Christina ever discussed racism was when Christina was concerned about potential encounters with racism.

Never anything serious [about race has come up], no. I mean I know that when she, she's married to a white man. And . . . when she first got engaged, that was sort of like weighing on her mind, you know. Like they were looking for apartments, and it's like, you know, some people might look at them and be like "Oh, it's an interracial couple." And that might, you know, pose problems for them to get an apartment or something like that. The way people would look at them might be a little difficult. In terms of that, we've talked about it. But in terms of her and me being friends, that's never really come up, no. (Paula, white, 24)

Paula says that she and Christina rarely talk about race because "it's never really been an issue." She does not think that racial issues pertain to their "personal lives."

Christina, brought up by Caribbean immigrants in an urban, primarily black and working-class neighborhood, agrees that it wouldn't be "natural" for her and Paula to discuss racial issues often.

We can talk about it. And Paula and I can talk about the issue of race without a problem but it's not something that really comes up, we've got other things more, more pressing to talk about. (Christina, black, 24)

She says that race is not something that crosses her mind when looking at Paula.

It doesn't have to be in your face all the time because for me it does, it completely fades to the background. When I'm talking to Paula, I don't sit here thinking, "I'm talking to my white friend Paula." You know, I think "Oh, she looks nice today. Her hair looks nice today." If she's wearing her nice pants. Anything. I mean, but I, I don't sit here thinking, "Oh, she's white." It's, it's beyond that. (Christina, black, 24)

Rather than bringing her and Paula closer together, she thinks that discussions of racial issues would be artificial and needlessly "divisive." Neither is very "politically minded," with any desire to, in Paula's words, "rehash" the topic of "racial equality or inequality" with one another.

Elizabeth and Louise, both middle-class professionals and natives of southern California, only discuss race during national news events such as the O.J. Simpson murder trial. As Louise describes it,

The only time we really got into something about race was during the O.J. Simpson trial and I thought he was not guilty and she thought he was guilty. . . . So, you know, we kind of—we discussed it for a while. And I told her my side, she told me her side— "And, aw, forget it. Let's go on to something else"—and then we talked about something else. (Louise, black, 45)

While Louise and Elizabeth are very comfortable with one another, the O.J. Simpson trial provided one of the very few occasions where race entered into their friendship. When asked, individually, if race is ever an issue in their friendship, both brought up their discussion of O.J.'s guilt or innocence. Neither Louise nor Elizabeth agreed with the other's view and both realized that their disagreement was race-based. Like most white Americans, Elizabeth believed that he was guilty, and like the majority of black Americans, Louise believed that he was innocent.[6] However, they simply chose to agree to disagree and talk "about something else," rather than continue it and highlight the racial division that existed between them.

Mary and Patrice are also examples of white and black friends who rarely discuss race. They met when Mary, a professor at a large midwestern university, volunteered to tutor at the after-school center Patrice attended. Even the few discussions they had about race that centered on the rather light topics of which cosmetics or clothes would best suit each other's coloring took some time to develop. As their relationship grew, Mary became a mentor and, eventually, a friend of Patrice's outside the tutoring center. Their conversations about race then became more relaxed. When asked whether their discussions about race have changed from the early stages of their friendship, Mary replied:

Yeah, because now we're friends. At some point, we made a transition [to] where . . . she knew that I liked her, so I felt more comfortable letting myself think she wouldn't misinterpret it. So I became less cautious. . . . You know, so, I guess we're comfortable talking about our race as it affects, as it relates to beauty or cosmetic issues or clothing issues. (Mary, white, 38)

Mary also mentioned that, in her now secondary role as a mentor for Patrice, they have talked about the importance of some cultural aspects of race, such as how important it is for Patrice to participate more fully in church life. Overall, however, the pair rarely discuss race. When asked whether she and Mary talk much about racial issues, Patrice, who grew up in a predominantly poor, urban, African American neighborhood in the Midwest said "Actually no. . . .

I feel like it doesn't matter. You know, you can be purple, green, or brown and still have a lot of things in common." It is on those things they have in common that Patrice and Mary, and most of the other pairs of friends, focus.

Dave and Kofi, two middle-class professionals in their mid-thirties who have been best friends since meeting at their New England college, never discuss race. When asked whether the topic of race comes up much between him and his friend Dave, Kofi, a native of Africa who came to the United States as a boy, said:

No, it doesn't. . . . Hey, I know he's a Caucasian man. I know that. And I'm sure that he sees me as an African American person. But we don't. There are no issues. I mean, we don't talk about race per se. I can't even think of any one thing that we've talked about in terms of race. Because it's just—You know, we're friends. That's where it is. That's the way it is. (Kofi, black, 35)

Dave, who grew up in a predominantly white New England neighborhood, echoed Kofi's statement when he tried to explain why he and Kofi do not discuss racial issues.

Certainly it's not anything that I consciously avoided. I think we. I don't know, we're just two shallow guys. I don't know. [laughs] I don't know. Again, certainly, it's not anything that was consciously not brought up on my part. It's just ah, never been an issue with us. (Dave, white, 35)

The responses that both Kofi and Dave give to the question about whether they discuss race in their friendship reveals their unease with the topic. While Dave jokes that they just must be "two shallow guys" for not talking about race, Kofi describes him as the opposite of shallow, "not the kind of person that says a lot but . . . does things." Best friends since college, both men take their friendship very seriously and are clearly committed to one another. They have discussed extremely personal issues with each other and, as Kofi says, Dave is "not the type to open up [but] he opened up [to me]." Somehow, though, without conscious effort, the two have never discussed the issue that divides so many black and white Americans from one another—race. Just as platonic cross-sex friends deemphasize sexuality when they're together, Kofi and Dave, like the majority of the interracial friends, have deemphasized race in their relationship.

JOKING ABOUT RACE

Ignoring or limiting discussions of race is one means of dealing with the "elephant in the living room." However, there are some pairs of friends who turn to their racial differences with humor as a means of cementing their relationships. The first time one makes fun of the other with a racial joke or slur and receives a good-humored, similarly racist and abusive response, they know their friendship is on solid ground. These pairs of friends trade incessant racial barbs, yet rarely have a serious discussion about race or racial issues. Communication experts would not be surprised to learn that this is most common among young male pairs of friends.

Nine of the forty pairs of friends fall chiefly into this category of black-white friends. Instead of generally ignoring the topic, this group deals with the issue of race by hurling racial insults at one another. Six of these pairs of friends consist of young men now in college. Three pairs of women also bring up race primarily through joking, though they also discuss individual incidents of racism that they have either faced or noticed.

Joe and Devin represent this second way that close black-white friends may deal with the issue of race. Joe, raised in a primarily white upper-middle-class New York suburb, aptly sums up the role race plays in these friendships by saying

You know, when I look at friendships in general or specifically my friendship with Devin, it's amazing how much race plays a role, but doesn't play a role. How much we joke about it, but we never talk about it seriously. (Joe, black, 18)

To them, racial stereotypes can be used as "in" jokes that bring them closer together. In many ways, their interactions are similar to those of the interracial buddy/partner characters Mel Gibson and Danny Glover play in the series of *Lethal Weapon* movies. As Devin, who grew up in a middle-class, predominantly white New England town describes it

We make a weird fun of each other's ethnic backgrounds so much; it's incredible. . . . Like we found each other's stereotypes—I'm Irish and German—so we're, we're pretty bad with it. . . . Like I saw him at lunch, we were eating, and I saw him come back from one of the meal booths . . . and I was like, "What you got there—some fried chicken and Koolade?" [He, in turn, might say something like] "Why don't you build a new gas chamber? (Devin, white, 18)

Aware that people overhearing them are often aghast, Joe and Devin joke with each other in ways that they would never joke with others. They also readily admit that they would never permit others, outside their close circle of friends, to joke either with themselves or their close friend in a similar manner. Each expressed a strong willingness to defend their friend from any racial insults that others might deliver.

Vern and James, college students who both grew up in lower-middle-class New Jersey neighborhoods with increasing numbers of blacks, also use the topic of race as fodder for put-downs of one another. When asked whether race has ever come up or been an issue in their friendship, Vern's succinct response was:

No, not at all. Except for when we're, like, ripping on each other. (Vern, white, 18)

When asked the same question, separately, James's response was almost identical to Vern's:

Just like joking. We always joke about people's races all the time. (James, black, 18)

Like Joe and Devin, and the majority of the young male interracial friends, Vern and James use racial jokes as a means of both bonding and acknowledging the "elephant in the living room" without having to address, with any depth, the fact that race affects them both in different ways.

While in some friendship pairs the line may seem very far off, there is a line that the friends know to avoid crossing when joking with one another. As Steven describes it,

Well, you know, we talk about stuff, mostly joking. And, you know, it's a really open kind of friendship. You know, I'll say things and, you know, he'll say things and whenever those lines are crossed we know, you know, all you have to do is say "I'm not comfortable with that." And he backs off and I back off.

When asked who crosses the line more often, Steven said,

On the issue of race? It's probably him crossing the line and me telling him that that's not something I'm comfortable with. But, I mean, it doesn't happen often. But, on the other hand, I don't think I've ever crossed a racial line with him, you know. And that just goes with the whole, you know, I think it's more serious . . . saying things that are offensive towards black people than it is saying things that are offensive towards white people. I guess it's just kind of society today. (Steven, black, 19)

The different locations of the white and black "no crossing" line when it comes to racial jokes has nothing to do with political correctness. Young men who insult each other with as much wit and effort to disgust one another as these young men are not bound by current "adult" rules of verbal etiquette in their exchanges with one another. In some ways, they are carrying on the time-honored tradition of disparaging one another that male youths have acted out with each other for centuries.[7] Those who manage to deliver the most outrageous insults, while avoiding hitting a spot that is a little too sensitive and could start a fight, gain in stature among their friends.[8]

The reason that blacks are more sensitive than whites to racial jokes is intimately connected with the fact that blacks have been the butt of racial slurs and jokes associated with their devaluation, dehumanization, and lynching[9] throughout the history of the United States. Today, as a group, blacks are still socially, politically, and economically in lower standing than whites. Whites, as a racial group, on the other hand, have not faced such abuse and still hold disproportionate economic, political, and social power in the United States. Just as it is easier to bear a "you are so ugly" joke when you are relatively good looking, it is much easier to take a racial insult when your race is in a position of power relative to those hurling the insults.

The fact that both friends feel comfortable, on the whole, trading race-based insults with one another is a sign of their closeness, despite their racial differences. Trading jokes and insults can also give the surface impression that the two friends are on an equal playing field. The only indication that the field is still slanted is the fact that racial insults are more likely to injure the black friend than the white one.

SERIOUSLY DISCUSSING RACE

The friends who openly discuss the different positions of blacks and whites in society represent the third category of responses to the issue of race. These friends directly comment, with great seriousness, on the "elephant in the living room." Eleven of the friendship pairs have discussed race at length. They were deeply interested, usually near the beginning of their friendships, in discovering all that they could about their friends' different racial background and perspective. Typically, the discussions would begin with the white friend asking the black friend questions. However, the conversations would almost always include multiple exchanges of opinions and information.

With each pair, however, the topic of race arose less frequently as time went by.[10] In all friendships, the differences between the friends that first seemed novel become normal, and less of a conversation maker as the friendship develops. The black-white friends who spent hours learning from each other's experiences and opinions on racial issues toward the beginning of their friendships gradually turned to other topics as their friendships developed. After many years of friendship, the friends tended to talk about race only when discussing a news item or dealing with the racial issues of "others." Their lengthy talks about the subject earlier in their friendships often enable them to now feel confident that they know the other's thoughts on a current racial event or issue without having to ask.

Evan and Bob, friends now for many years, illustrate the third way in which many black-white friends deal with issues of race over time. While they eagerly discussed issues of race when they first became friends, their conversations now tend to focus on other topics. As Evan states,

> Well, I can tell you, Bob and I [spent] a lot of time just talking about race. Differences and attitudes, you know, things like that. . . . So, we've done a lot of exploring, he and I. Just questioning each other and talking in general. [But] we have a tendency now to focus on the similarities, instead of the differences. . . . We don't talk about it too much anymore now because we're past that. We've asked all the questions we want to ask. Or we've covered that ground and we know the answer.
>
> [However], I would still not hesitate at all if a question came up about race or something like that. In fact, I've often thought to myself, if I ever have a problem, with an African American employee, I'll call Bob first and run it by him to get his view on it before I took any action. (Evan, white, 41)

So while they have already "covered that ground," Evan and Bob have not decided to simply ignore race now. Instead, it has become just one of the many reasons, like guidance on work issues, jogging, and marital issues, for which they might turn to each other for advice. Evan and Bob value each other on multiple levels and embrace the many identities, including racial, of each.

In some ways like Evan and Bob, Caroline turned to Janet for a sounding board when she dealt with issues of race in her work life. When Caroline, a white, upper-middle-class midwestern professor and professional consultant, first started work at a company that, aside from her, was virtually all black, she was grateful to find her assistant, Janet, very willing to guide her through what for her was a new cultural environment. When asked how often she and Janet had discussions about racial issues, Caroline said,

I think early on, a lot. You know, like typically every day something would be coming up. . . . Because I was surrounded, for the first time in my life, with African American women, working in [this] setting. And I truly wanted to understand their point of view. And I would say that Janet was sort of a, um, a critical person in helping me to understand a world that I had never experienced before. She was much more savvy in that world of employees that we had to work with that had problems and our clients, our residents, and their families. . . . I mean, she was absolutely indispensable in helping me learn cultural ins and outs. (Caroline, white, 53)

Through the trust and rapport they developed through working together, Janet and Caroline have become very close friends and "part of one another's family" over the ten years they have known each other. Their relationship is markedly different from the hierarchical workplace relationships between whites and blacks that Hudson and Hines-Hudson described. While Caroline was, in reality, Janet's superior in the hierarchical structure of their company, Caroline repeatedly described their working relationship in terms that stressed their collaborative efforts. In the workplace Caroline depended upon Janet's willingness to share her knowledge of black culture. The fact that Caroline treated Janet as an equal at work in some ways balanced the playing field and most likely contributed to the ease with which their close friendship developed.

Caroline and Janet's experience was rare. Approximately four-fifths of the friendship pairs in this sample are composed of two people with similar educational and economic backgrounds. However, more than most other pairs of friends in this sample, the support Caroline and Janet gave each other dealing with issues of race was mutual. Because Janet was Caroline's assistant when they first met, and Caroline was educationally and financially in a superior situation, she was able to provide Janet much guidance and support in attaining further degrees in higher education and negotiating the predominantly white corporate world.

Typically among the friendship pairs, the teaching about culture was primarily one-sided. Black people, living in a white-dominated society, are usually much more knowledgeable about white culture than whites are of black culture and therefore have less need of a tutorial about the other race. They, in many ways, must be bicultural, able to live in both black and white worlds. W. E. B. DuBois described this as having a "double consciousness" in *The Souls of Black*

Folk.[11] Whites, on the other hand, while they may be fans of Michael Jordan and the Wayans brothers, do not often look into everyday black America. In the pairs in which race was an open topic, the white interviewees spoke appreciatively of their friends' assistance in their efforts to learn and understand the cultural differences between many black and white Americans.

Given the American obsession with race, one might think that the vast majority of close black-white friends would discuss racial issues often. Yet, the overwhelming majority of friendship pairs (97.5 percent) did not make race the centerpiece of their friendships. Even pairs who have serious discussions about racism in U.S. society concentrate on other aspects of their friendships. Rod describes this phenomenon within his friendship with Vinnie.

I think race died down a long time ago in Vinnie's and my relationship. Now, it's personal. [laughs] It's just personal. You know, this is so corny. I know he's a white guy, you know, and he knows I'm a black guy. But that's not a part of if. It's just the blood we've shed. You know, and the tears we've cried. I don't think it is. It just doesn't come up anymore except when talking about others and their deal with race. And how we see some people just doing some stupid things. And that's when, you know, they'll get our hair up. . . . Like we won't tolerate racial insensitivity or anything like that on our team. But it wouldn't manifest itself because, cause we're there. You know. So, I think, in response to "does race come up?" it comes up when dealing with others but not when dealing with each other. (Rod, black, 45)

Having grown completely comfortable with the racial differences between them, their attention toward race now focuses outward. Through the example of their friendship, and the way they coach together, Rod and Vinnie show their players and those around them that close friendships can be formed across the racial divide.

WHEN THE TOPIC OF RACE EXPLODES

Only one of the pairs made race a center of their friendship. And that center is now unstable. Hillary and Doris dealt with race in a manner that is atypical of close black-white friends. Unlike the other friendship pairs, they made race the focus of their relationship. Their conversations on race were purposive, rather than naturally derived during the course of their friendship.

While an anomaly, the friendship of Hillary and Doris is worth exploring for the number of "hot button" racial issues that the two actively dealt with very early in their friendship. Their story is also a sobering one that indicates that grappling with racial issues constantly early and often may severely harm an otherwise promising friendship.

When Hillary, raised in primarily upper-middle-class white settings in the United States and abroad, moved into Doris's primarily black neighborhood in a major northeastern city a little over a year before this interview, both were surprised and delighted to find how much they had in common. As Doris, raised in the lower working class but now an upper-middle-class professional, describes it,

There were so many things that were similar. We're the same age. . . . I'll be fifty this year. . . . Our husbands, you know, if they were the same color, they'd sound like the same man. . . . We both [have] three daughters. We're both in transition in terms of our careers. And so, it was just so much there that was natural for a friendship. (Doris, black, 49)

They began to chat daily as they walked their dogs together and quickly realized that, as Doris says, "there [was] very little difference between the two of us, the difference is color." Both writers, they decided to purposefully examine the issue of race in their relationship and write an article about what they discovered. Only a month into their relationship, instead of avoiding racial issues, they each began to hunt for them. Hillary and Doris's experiment quickly led to an increasing sense of both distance and friction between them. As Doris puts it,

I have friends that I've grown up with and they cross, you know, all different racial groups and backgrounds. But they, they were along friend lines and, so, if we dealt with race, it was in the most nonthreatening way. But here, we decided to take it head on and so there would be a tension. (Doris, black, 49)

While the article was published in a major magazine, the discussions on race became heated and began to take a toll on their friendship. As Hillary explained,

Oh, our first major blowout was when we had [the] article coming out. . . . I had a bit of a set-to with the black editor. . . . She wanted to take these things out of [my part of the piece] that were really telling. . . . And she was being impossible. And I went to the woman above her, who happens to be white, who I also know. And Doris . . . said . . . , "you know, this is what white people always do. They always go over the black person to the white person." And, you know, I would have gone over her head to the black person, if the person over her head had been black. But it's just sort of *every* situation is impossible, because it's looked at through a black and white lens. (Hillary, white, 50)

Doris echoed Hillary's description of the increasing tension in their relationship.

What we were experiencing was that, what I would think would be an innocuous statement [would be] a bomb to her and vice versa. And it was only [when] we said, you know when you said x, y, and z? This is how it impacted me, that we realized the depth of the racial divide. And it was and it is scary. (Doris, black, 49)

While Hillary thought Doris's desire for her children to attend black colleges was racially divisive and needlessly separatist, Doris felt that Hillary acted like "a pampered white woman." Doris admitted that she can sometimes see "race all the time," but maintained that Hillary's lack of racial awareness is an example of white privilege that infuriated her.

Hillary explained:

I guess it made me realize how deep the feelings go. And when I say how deep the feelings go, I mean for black people. One of the things I said that offended her when we were having our awful time [occurred when] I said something about, you need this more than I do. I said, I can go off back to my little white life and I don't have to, I don't have to sit and examine what's causing you to be, you know. And she came back with, "Of course this affects all of us." And I said, Yes, it affects all of us. And as Americans, we should all take it on. But the fact is, is that it affects you more than me because you're in the minority. And, I mean, I think that's true. [slight laugh] It's much more rare for me to walk in. I mean, it virtually never happens except at her house, to walk into a gathering where I'm in the minority. And so, I guess . . . my relationship with Doris has affected my feelings about race. It's given me a lot more understanding of how hard it is for them. (Hillary, white, 50)

Hillary's new appreciation for the struggles that blacks go through every day is something that most whites never think about. As Peggy MacIntosh illustrated,[12] whites benefit from whiteness being the "norm" in U.S. society in myriad ways that are often imperceptible to whites, from "flesh"-colored bandages matching white skin to the freedom from the pressures of always being viewed as a "representative" of their race. Paula Rothenberg, who shares her own gradual recognition of the benefits that come from her position as an upper-middle-class white American in *Invisible Privilege*, argues, like MacIntosh, that white Americans must make an effort to step out of their sense of normality in order to recognize their race-based privilege.[13]

Hillary's friendship with Doris made her cognizant of the fact that, in order to live a successful life in America, she does not have to find herself in situations where she is in the minority and viewed as "representing" all whites. Doris, on the other hand, a prominent lawyer in a major city, is viewed as "representing" blacks in predominantly white settings all the time. She has experienced white subordinates "going above her" to her white boss. The conversations and experiences with race these two friends shared inflamed Doris's racial wounds and left Hillary thinking that Doris was hypersensitive about issues of race.

For several months before this interview, Doris and Hillary consciously avoided dealing with issues of race with each other. Doris described how their arguments over race left a "wreckage" to which they do not yet wish to return.

I think the reason why we've not embraced racial issues [these past months] is because of our last venture down that dark alleyway. [laughs] In our last venture down, I mean, it was serious. I got sick, physically sick. We were yelling at each other. We didn't talk for at least a week. . . . [When she said that] she didn't feel about race the way I did . . . [and that] she could go back to her privileged white world with her privileged white friends and be perfectly happy. And didn't have to do this. I said, well, okay. That's honest. That's honest. And that was a level of honesty that we had not gotten to. And so, my hope was that, okay, let's work through this piece. But it was too deep. It was too deep. . . . I got really in touch with the whole notion of white privilege. Up front, in person, in black and white. [slight laugh] With that statement. Because . . . I thought, I think, we all have to do this. . . . And I looked at it and I said, now how could she say that? I know what her background is. I know the kinds of issues she went through. I know what she's going through now. And there's very little difference between the two of us. The difference is color. So, . . . I said, if you're privileged, does that make me unprivileged? And so we were getting to a level, I think that, well, it was explosive and exploded. It exploded and we've not yet been back to the wreckage [slight laugh] frankly. Because I do think we got in touch with a very significant piece about white privilege. So, I guess we've not been back to the wreckage of that last piece because it was, I think it was, so at the core of race issues. (Doris, black, 49)

Since that time, Hillary and Doris still talk, but are not as open with each other as they once were. As Hillary says,

We still get together most mornings, with our dogs. But we've kept it on a pretty superficial level. (Hillary, white, 50)

Both have feelings of trepidation about renewing their discussions about race. As Doris describes it,

We have gone through some real heated times, to the point where we've both been burned. And so there's a sensitivity to exposed burned skin. (Doris, 49, black)

Neither Doris nor Hillary wants to be burned by race again.

However, as evidenced by their willingness to be interviewed as a pair of "close friends" for this book, both Hillary and Doris maintain that they would like to have the closeness with each other they began to feel before these discussions came between them. As Doris says, "there's too much of us that's so similar" not to be friends. The only uncertainty is whether they can repair the damage that their arguments about race inflicted on their developing friendship. The majority of the close friends in the sample, even those who have been friends for many years, do not seriously discuss racial issues. Without the protection of a history of shared good times and mutual support, Doris and Hillary leapt headlong into serious personal discussions about race and emerged bruised and wary of more injury. Having brought race to the forefront of their friendship before the relationship was more secure, their friendship may have been permanently damaged. Both would like to repair it but fear further harm if they go near the topic that drove them apart—race.

Unlike Doris and Hillary, all the other friendship pairs have managed to successfully and safely manage the potentially volatile topic of race in their friendship. At this time, none appears to be on shaky ground. However, there is no way of telling how many black-white friendships once existed or started to develop only to be cut down by disagreements over racial issues. While all the other pairs in this sample managed to deal with the "elephant in the living room" in a manner that preserved their friendships, Doris and Hillary may be the tip of an iceberg invisible to this study.

Doris's and Hillary's frank discussions about race bring to light the fact that most white and black Americans are divided over issues of race. For example, a 2001 Gallup poll revealed that while four out of ten white people say that blacks are treated "the same as" whites, only one out of ten blacks maintain that blacks and whites are treated equally in the United States.[14] As sociologist Herbert Gans said upon hearing the results of this poll,

It is very hard if you are in the majority to understand how the minority is treated. It is very hard for whites to understand what it is like to be told every 30 seconds that you are not good enough and that you can't be trusted. Things like when you go shopping downtown and all of a sudden all the doors are locked, or when you step outside . . . to catch a taxicab and you can't get one. It's something very hard for whites to imagine.[15]

Hints of both Hillary's and Doris' different outlooks on race and the results of the Gallup poll appear throughout the other friendship dyads.

Instead of using the strategies of topic avoidance, joking about racial issues, or waiting to have serious discussions about race until their friendship was on a relatively firm foundation like the other interviewees did, Hillary and Doris exposed their different perspectives on race early in their relationship. While they did so in a way that is artificial, and not customary in the development of close black-white friendships, the differences that their experiment exposed are very real. Black and white Americans cannot see racial issues in the same way because they view them from different perspectives.

As described in chapter 1, the outlooks that blacks and whites have on racial issues differ as a result of the continuing inequality between whites and blacks in the United States. The different levels of resistance that blacks and whites feel against cross-racial friendships discussed in chapter 2 stem directly from the historic and present discrimination faced by blacks. The fact that the majority of close black-white friends do not seriously discuss issues of race is a testimony to the still painful and volatile separation that exists between black and white Americans. Doris and Hillary provide a sobering example of just how explosive and damaging issues of race can be when brought to the center of the relationship of close black-white friends.

In their own ways, interracial friends develop strategies to keep race from consuming their friendships. The typical means, topic avoidance, is successful through the efforts of both the white and the black individuals in each of the pairs. However, the reasons why each of the friends so rarely brings up issues of race in the context of their relationship vary with the race of the friend. Chapter 4 takes a closer look at why and how so many blacks and whites in close interracial friendships do not talk about race.

NOTES

1. Walid Affifi and Laura Guerrero, "Some Things Are Better Left Unsaid II: Topic Avoidance in Friendships," *Communication Quarterly* 46, 3 (1998): 231–49.

2. See M. Monsour, B. Harris, N. Kurzweil, and C. Beard, "Challenges Confronting Cross-Sex Friendships: 'Much Ado About Nothing?'" *Sex Roles* 31 (1994): 55–77; M. R. Parks and K. Floyd, "Meanings for Closeness and Intimacy in Friendship," *Journal of Social and Personal Relationships* 13 (1996): 85–107; V. J. Derlega, S. Metts, S. Petronio, and S. T. Margulis, *Self-Disclosure*. Newbury Park, CA: Sage Publications, 1993.

3. Laura Guerrero and Walid Affifi, "Some Things Are Better Left Unsaid: Topic Avoidance in Family Relationships," *Communication Quarterly* 43 (1995): 276–96; Affifi and Guerrero, "Some Things II."

4. Affifi and Guerrero, "Some Things II."

5. Wendy Samter and William Cupach, "Friendly Fire: Topical Variations in Conflict Among Same and Cross-Sex Friends," *Communication Studies* 49, 42 (1998): 124.

6. Frank Newport and Lydia Saad, "Civil Trial Didn't Alter Public's View of Simpson Case," *Gallup News Service*, Feb. 7, 1997. Accessed at http://www.gallup.com/poll /releases/pr970207.asp.

7. Shakespeare provided an illustration of such behavior in *Romeo and Juliet* c. 1598.

8. One of the anonymous reviewers pointed out that "this ritual is referred to in the black community as 'playing the dozens.' Hitting the hot spot usually means saying something derogatory about someone's mother."

9. The fact that these types of jokes are still told is evident in the fact that one white twenty-four-year-old interviewee related a joke her boyfriend recently heard as follows: "This one guy goes, 'I have no problem with black people. I've got one in my family tree.' And, and then someone goes 'Oh, really,' and he goes, 'Yeah, he's hanging in my backyard.'" She was appalled both by the joke and that people could still be so "stupid" and "ignorant."

10. One pair, who met in grade school and are now in their late twenties, did not seriously discuss their different thoughts and experiences of race until they were in college. Since that time, they have followed the trend of the other pairs in this category and have talked about racial issues less often as time passes.

11. W. E. B. DuBois, *The Souls of Black Folk: Essays and Sketches* (Greenwich, CT: Fawcett, 1961).

12. Peggy McIntosh, "White Privilege: Unpacking the Invisible Knapsack," *Peace and Freedom*, July–Aug. 1989, pp. 10–12.

13. Paula Rothenberg, *Invisible Privilege: A Memoir About Race, Class, and Gender* (Lawrence: University Press of Kansas, 2000).

14. Gallup Organization, "Special Reports: Black–White Relations in the United States, 2001 Update," July 10, 2001. Accessed at http://www.gallup.com/poll/reports /bwr2001/sr010711.asp.

15. Matthew Valia, "Cultural Disconnect: How Whites, Blacks View Race in America," *DiversityInc.com*, July 10, 2001. Accessed at http://www.diversityinc.com/inside articlepg.cfm?SubMenuID=330&ArticleID=3387&CFIL.

4

Distancing Racism from the Friendship

I'm kind of tripping myself up and not following my own logic but . . .
African Americans do have it more difficult and Kofi probably has in ways
I don't realize. . . . Maybe it's just something I really haven't given a lot
of thought to before, to be honest with you. I'm really thinking about that
for the first time now as we're speaking about it. . . . It's just not something
I've had to think about.

Dave, white, 35

Well, I think [Dave's] advantaged over me due to race. Yah. But, you know,
he didn't ask for it. [laughs] He was born and it like just happened.

Kofi, black, 35

When William Julius Wilson wrote *The Declining Significance of Race*[1] in
1978, he argued that, as the black middle class grew through affirmative action
programs, economic stratification became a more divisive factor than race in
American society. Since that time, however, as many advocates of "colorblind"
policies have denounced race-based affirmative action programs, Wilson has
pointed out the continued need to acknowledge and take into account the disadvantages blacks experience today as a result of racism. In his 1999 article
"Affirming Opportunity,"[2] Wilson stressed that whites still have advantages
over even middle-class blacks. As noted throughout the previous chapters, evidence of persistent racial discrimination abounds in the United States.

Most Americans acknowledge that racism is still prevalent in the United
States. A 2001 Gallup poll revealed that 62 percent of whites and 91 percent
of blacks maintain that blacks are treated "not very well" or "badly" in the
United States.[3] While it is not surprising that more blacks than whites believe
that blacks face negative treatment, almost two-thirds of whites recognize that
racism exists in the United States. One might assume, then, that members of
black-white close friendships would be well aware that the white friend has
race-based privileges that the black friend does not.

The inequality between whites and blacks today brings unique challenges to cross-racial friendships. No matter how similar they may be in other respects or how fond of each other they are, these friends must somehow deal with the fact that they are members of racial groups that are treated differently in our society. This chapter focuses on how friends in relationships that cross the racial divide handle the race-based inequalities between them.

As a group, the white interviewees in this sample are more cognizant of racism in the United States than the average white American. All indicated that they were at least somewhat aware that racism is a problem in the U.S. However, while they all believe that racism is a societal issue, the majority of the white friends had a difficult time connecting racism in U.S. society to the experiences of their black friends. When asked whether they think either they or their friends have advantages over the other as a result race, almost three out of four said that they were not racially privileged in comparison to their black friends.

The black interviewees also tended to disassociate their white friends from the effects of racism in U.S. society. While all but three[4] of the black interviewees said that whites have an overall advantage in U.S. society, nine of the thirty-seven black interviewees who maintained that whites have an advantage over blacks said that their close white friends did not have a race-based advantage over them. Those who did state that their white friends had advantages over them distanced their white friends from any responsibility for the current racial disparities in the United States.

This tendency for the friends to put race "on a shelf," and distance racism from the friendship, both challenges and supports the traditional understanding of the concept of homophily. As noted in chapter 1, social psychologists who study friendship formation emphasize that most close friendships are formed on the basis of "like attracting like."[5] The ability of close black-white friends to focus on their commonalities, and either downplay or ignore the race-based differences between them, allows them to experience with each other the interpersonal attraction common among same-race close friends.

While this phenomenon indicates that the classic notion of homophily must be expanded to include interracial friendships, it also highlights the fact that friendships, like all relationships, are maintained through persistent efforts. For instance, two people may see similarities between themselves, be attracted to those commonalities, and become friends. During their friendship, in order to retain or increase that level of attraction, they must continually find ways to see each other as alike and avoid potential topics that might create distance between them.

As Erving Goffman noted in *Interaction Ritual*, each friend follows implicit rules of social interaction.[6] If one brings to light an uncomfortable difference between them or otherwise behaves inappropriately, "repair work" must be done. For instance, one can deal with burping in front of a friend by saying "excuse me" and continuing to carry on a conversation or making a joke out of it in order to "repair" the breech in social etiquette. Differences in racial privileges that are exposed in conversation between white and black friends can also be brushed over quickly or turned into fodder for jokes in order to assure both friends that race will not disturb the equilibrium between them.

While what Goffman called "impression management" takes place in all interactions, it is particularly important when major disparities exist between friends.[7] For instance, friends from different economic classes tend to avoid discussing their finances with one another for fear of creating tension. Many medical students and interns tend to discuss their work life only with colleagues, believing that friends outside the profession would not be able to relate. Often, young adults who marry and have children find they must make an effort to avoid constantly talking about their children and thereby alienate their single friends. The single friends and the parents may make jokes about the sudden differences in their lives, trying to keep or perhaps "repair" the bond with their friends through humor. Whatever strategy is employed, the goal of portraying themselves as similar remains constant.

While any pair of friends may choose to ignore or smooth over some of the differences between them, black and white friends face a special challenge to view themselves as similar in a society where race plays such a prominent and divisive role. Because race affects whites and blacks differently in U.S. society, black and white members of interracial dyads each have distinct ways of dealing with the race-based differences between them. Their different perspectives on race result from both these disparities.

THE WHITE VIEW

While every white interviewee acknowledged, to at least some extent, that racism exists in U.S. society today, only thirteen of the forty readily acknowledged their relative privilege in comparison to their black friends and to blacks in general. Their responses ranged from Caroline's critique of the "structural inequality . . . [that] disproportionately stack[s the deck] against children of color" to Paul's conviction that he is "at a huge advantage" over his friend Keith. Paul described how his foray into the business world with Keith helped him realize his relative privilege.

Sophomore year . . . we worked for Telefund again and we raised lots of money for school. And they asked us to go speak to the alumni about how to raise money. And we went in suits and in a limo to this big high-rise building [in a major city in the Northeast]. And we went in to talk to them. And they were all white. And the president of the university was white. And there's Keith. And I don't think any of them really opened up an eye or looked at him odd. But when we were all done, business cards got passed to me and people said, you know, "Give us a call" or do this or do that. And it wasn't done with Keith. . . . And since the . . . group [that] has most of the money in politics and control of the finance industry [is white], it feels comfortable with me there, and not with Keith. And I could care less but those doors then get open to me. (Paul, white, 22)

While Paul "could care less" about skin color, the reaction of the businesspeople at the meeting at which he and Keith spoke made it very clear to him that his white skin gave him an advantage over his black friend.

The majority of the white interviewees, however, were either reluctant to say or simply unaware that race gave them an advantage over their black friends. This was true even when they shared stories of witnessing their friends face discrimination. While only four white interviewees completed the interview still firmly believing that they do not have any race-based privileges over their friends, none of the twenty-seven who initially denied their advantage indicated that they had ever previously compared their own racial privileges with those of their friends. Most, like Matt, a nineteen-year-old white college student, revealed that they had far less trouble seeing racism as a societal issue than as a problem for their black friends.

Matt acknowledged that whites, as a group, are "holding all the cards" in U.S. society. He also described how he makes a point of talking to black people, in an effort to bridge the racial divide. However, he did not see that his race gives him an advantage over his black friend. Matt's response to the question of whether race plays a factor in how people are treated in the United States today was typical of someone with this tunnel vision on issues of race. Asked whether he sees Chris as having any advantages over him as a result of race, he responded

No, And if I have any over him, I guess it's just more of a class thing. But. You know, I like to think we're on an equal playing field.

He continued, with some equivocation

For the most part. . . . I should hope [we're on an equal playing field]. . . . I would think so. I mean I would [treat us equally] if I were the boss. But then again I'm not. (Matt, white, 19)

However, when asked again whether he believes that he and Chris are both on a relatively even playing field, Matt responded with an affirmative "mmmhmm." While Matt recognizes the larger social issue of racism, he does not link it to his friend Chris's individual life.

Like Matt, the majority of the white interviewees easily recognized racism on a societal level but had a difficult time seeing that racism affected their friends. For instance, after saying that his friend Kofi does not have "any particular advantage or disadvantage over me because of his race," Dave stated that "generally speaking, on a societal level, black people may have it tougher" than whites. When asked why Kofi does not have it tougher, Dave perceived the illogic in his thinking.

Why wouldn't Kofi have it tougher? Maybe he has but he's just overcome. Because why wouldn't he, right? It's just so funny, I mean, I just see Kofi and he's just—He's Kofi, he's not the black Kofi. I don't know, that's odd. Yah. I'm kind of tripping myself up and not following my own logic but . . . African Americans do have it more difficult and Kofi probably has in ways I don't realize. . . . He's probably had to work harder than I or anyone else probably realizes to get there. . . . Maybe it's just something I really haven't given a lot of thought to before, to be honest with you. I'm really thinking about that for the first time now as we're speaking about it. . . . It's just not something I've had to think about. (Dave, white, 35)

Dave, while being a very close and loyal friend to Kofi for more than fifteen years, has somehow managed to avoid thinking about how racism affects his black friend. While he can recognize that racism exists in U.S. society, he had, up until the moment of the interview, never thought about how if affected Kofi. He echoes Rothenberg in *Invisible Privilege* when he says, "it's just not something I've had to think about."[8]

Peggy, too, had a hard time relating the racism that she perceives at the societal level to her friend Ese's experiences. During the interview, she first said that she thought she and Ese have an equal chance of "making it" in society, despite their different races. She then stated that more white people discriminate against blacks than vice versa. When questioned about the two statements, she, like Dave, quickly realized her inconsistency as she responded.

Hmmm. . . . I think that we have an equal chance but she has. . . . I think that she's more likely to be discriminated against than I would be. Yah.

When prompted to explain how things are equal, Peggy laughed, realizing her contradiction, and said,

I guess they aren't. Yah. So yah. I guess that I have a higher chance of making it than she does.

Peggy stated that she had never thought about the race-based inequality between Ese and her, saying,

I guess I try to not think about things like that. . . . Um. I guess to protect her. And that's weird that I wouldn't think about it to protect her. Wow! What thoughts are running through my head! [laughs] Yah. I guess, you know, cause I don't want to see her hurt. So, I guess I just try not to think it. And maybe . . . because I think she can do anything. And so I'm in her mindset, too. You know, we share so much, I guess I'm thinking, well, I know what her plans are and what she's going to do and I don't see anything getting in her way. So, I guess that probably has the most to do with it. [I would like not to think] that she would ever have anybody say anything or be discriminatory against her at all. (Peggy, white, 21)

Just as Dave has pride in Kofi's ability to succeed, Peggy likes to believe that nothing will hinder Ese's attempts to fulfill her aspirations. Peggy doesn't *want* to think about how Ese may suffer from racism because the thought pains her. She doesn't *have* to think about it because she is white.

Moreover, Peggy does not recognize the benefits that come with being white. As they are for most white Americans, the advantages from her white skin are what Rothenberg refers to as invisible privileges.[9] Frankenberg explains that "among the effects on white people both of race privilege and of the dominance of whiteness are their seeming normativity, their structured invisibility."[10] Peggy's membership in the dominant race makes her privileges seemingly normal rather than noticeable to her.

Ellen, a fifty-nine-year-old white woman who grew up in a small, segregated town in the South, also had difficulty recognizing the racial discrimination that her friend Pam has faced. When asked whether either she or Pam has advantages over the other as a result of race, Ellen replied,

Pam probably has the advantage because she has the education and I don't. I mean, she could take care of herself. She can make money hand over fist because of the things she does. So, she actually has the advantage.

Asked whether the situation would be the same if they had a similar educational background, Ellen continued to dismiss the influence of race.

Well, Pam has made her own advantages by working hard. I think she doesn't allow anybody to make any difference. . . . I feel like she's never even thought about it.

However, when asked in a follow-up question whether she thinks that Pam has been completely exempted from racial discrimination, Ellen began to acknowledge that race has influenced Pam's experiences.

Oh, I'm sure she has [faced racial discrimination]. I'm sure she has. Maybe not so much now. I'm sure she has. She said her class was the class that integrated [her city's] public schools. (Ellen, white, 59)

Ellen then elaborated with an example:

I have seen a couple of things. . . . [For instance,] we walked into this little shop and I'm walking around and suddenly I see this old woman following Pam around. And we're just browsing but she's following Pam. And I think she suspected Pam because she was black. And I felt so uncomfortable. (Ellen, white, 59)

Ellen's contradictory answers are indicative of how hard it is for her to imagine, even when directly confronted with evidence of it, that her bright, successful friend could be harmed by racism.

These white interviewees are not obtuse about racism, however. As seen above, most eventually noticed the dissonance between their knowledge of racism in U.S. society and their stated lack of privilege as white people. However, while almost all admitted, at least partially, that whites have a race-based advantage over blacks, most viewed their friends as being on a par with themselves. Bill's description of how he and his white friends view his black friend Steven provides a good example of this mode of thinking.

We all get along just as if we were all, you know, all the same. Where it's very equal. I see Steven as a very equal person. I don't view him higher than me. I don't view him lower than me. (Bill, white, 19)

While Bill acknowledges in another part of the interview that he would "probably" have greater race-based privileges than Steven, he and Steven, like all but three of the other pairs of interviewees (the exceptions are the two pairs that began through a teacher-tutor relationship and the pair assigned to each other as roommates), were attracted to each other as like people are attracted to one other. The overwhelming majority of the pairs were drawn to one another by commonalities (e.g., same workplace, same college). This held true even for the three pairs from different economic classes. While all the white interviewees are at least somewhat aware that race, as the historian Manning Marable describes it, is "an unequal relationship between social aggregates,"[11] this knowledge rarely, if ever, enters into their thoughts about their black friends. The majority of these friends focus on their similarities and keep the friendship a safe distance from issues of race and racism.

Only four white interviewees, even when pressed, maintained clear opinions that they did not have advantages over their black friends as a result of race. All four, however, described in vivid detail episodes they witnessed of racial discrimination against blacks. In spite of relating these experiences, they remained firmly convinced, throughout the interview, that they did not have greater race-based privileges than their black friends. For example, Kristin, a white woman in her mid-thirties, grew up at the very center of the busing riots in Boston. She recounted what life was like during the turmoil and violence over busing.

I was old enough to remember Daryl Wiggins. He was a young black boy that was probably about fifteen or sixteen years old and he was a star football player. And he was on the football field practicing after school . . . and they went up on the roof and shot him, paralyzed him. It was really tough. It was . . . scary. I would wake up in the middle of the night and there would be bonfires going in the middle of the street. And when the tactical police force came down, they would have fishing wire across the street that would knock the cops right off their motorcycles. I grew up in a very tough time when it came to racial tension. (Kristin, white, 37)

Kristin's brother, who lives in a southern state, has told her that he and some of his black friends were recently thrown out of bars because of the race of his friends. Kristin believes, however, that this type of treatment varies from community to community and that whites are subject to similar racial discrimination when in some predominantly black settings.

Mary Anne's friendship with her black roommate, Vanessa, opened her eyes to present-day racism but still left her blind to some aspects of it. She described the time that she and Vanessa were followed at the mall as an experience that made her realize that racism still exists in the United States.

I know I've heard about like how blacks still don't really believe that they're really being accepted in this country. . . . I heard about like how when they go in stores and sometimes the sales person will follow them around. And I'm just like, you know, maybe they're just exaggerating. But actually, me and Vanessa went to the mall a couple of months ago [and] when we went into the store the sales lady was following us around. . . . And I'm like, "Vanessa, what's her problem? What is she doing? We're not doing anything." She's like "No, it's because of me." And I was just like "Really?" So we just kept walking around and she would just like follow us everywhere. So, we went around the corner and we were looking at a rack of clothes and the lady was like right around the corner *staring* at us. So I'm just like, "This is ridiculous. I'm just going to leave." I was going to say something to her. And Vanessa's like, "Oh, *no. Don't* say anything. . . . It happens all the time. I've just learned to ignore it."
But I was just—I really didn't think that that kind of thing happened anymore. . . . It made me angry. It really did. Because I thought that we [had] passed all that. (Mary Anne, white, 18)

Mary Anne recognizes that Vanessa has faced racial discrimination, yet she still clings to the notion that she, as a white person, does not have an advantage over her black friend.

I think that she kind of [has advantages over me] because she's a minority here. They try so hard to get them. . . . They put on all these programs and stuff for them. She's got minority-based scholarships and stuff like that which, I mean, I would never be able to get. . . . She doesn't really have any disadvantages that I know. (Mary Anne, white, 18)

Even after having witnessed discrimination against Vanessa, Mary Anne believes that Vanessa is not disadvantaged because of her race. In fact, Mary Anne concludes that, because of affirmative action programs, it is *she*, rather than Vanessa, who is underprivileged because of race.

Mary Anne's ability to maintain that she does not have race-based advantages over Vanessa, despite having seen, firsthand, Vanessa face discriminatory treatment exemplifies what Joe Feagin and Hernán Vera refer to as sincere fictions. According to Feagin and Vera, people create "sincere fictions" when they create "personal mythologies that reproduce societal mythologies at the individual level."[12] Mary Anne has taken the popular belief among whites that affirmative action programs unfairly benefit blacks at the expense of whites[13] and applied it to her and Vanessa's experience of race-based discrimination. This belief overpowers Mary Anne's knowledge that Vanessa has been directly hurt by racism and allows her to sincerely believe that it is she, rather than Vanessa, who faces race-based disadvantages.
Almost all the white interviewees stated that blacks benefit from affirmativeaction programs. Only Kristin, Mary Anne, and two other white interviewees, however, were convinced that whites do not have an overall race-based

advantage in the United States. The slights both Kristin and Mary Anne have felt from affirmative action programs appear to have colored their view on racism in the United States. Kristin was one of only two interviewees who described with certainty that they were denied an opportunity because of an affirmative action policy.[14] She related how, as a teenager, she was rejected by a prestigious high school at the same time that a black student who scored lower on the entrance exam was accepted. Kristin still feels strongly about that missed opportunity. Mary Anne also expressed some resentment over Vanessa's "minority-based scholarships and stuff like that which [she] would never be able to get."

As noted earlier, 62 percent of white Americans maintain that blacks are treated "not very well" or "badly," which implies that almost four out of ten believe that blacks are dealt with fairly in U.S. society today. Indeed, many white Americans now believe that so-called "reverse racism" is more of a problem than white racism. Some use this term when they point to personal incidents when they have been treated unfairly or harmed by individual blacks, such as being ignored by a black sales clerk or beaten up on a playground by a group of black youth shouting antiwhite slurs. They maintain that these painful episodes in their lives indicate that black-on-white racism ("reverse racism") or discrimination ("reverse discrimination") is just as harmful as the racial injustices blacks have traditionally faced. However, most white Americans use these labels when describing affirmative action programs.[15] According to a 2001 Gallup poll, 33 percent of whites maintain that affirmative action programs should be decreased.[16] All the white interviewees who either denied that or were initially unsure whether they had a race-based advantage over their friends mentioned affirmative action in their answers. They all maintained that affirmative action programs unfairly assisted blacks at the expense of whites.

The white interviewees' lack of awareness of white privilege is far from unique and not solely a result of the perceived inequities in affirmative action programs. It stems, in part, from the growing trend of so-called colorblindness discussed in chapter 2. Ashley Doane's term for this phenomenon among whites is "hidden ethnicity." As he understands it, "in terms of ethnic self-awareness, hidden ethnicity captures the reality that, for dominant group members [i.e., whites], ethnicity does not generally intrude upon day-to-day experience and that the privileges of group membership are taken for granted."[17]

Instead of feeling privileged, most white people have the sense, as Doane states, of "being the 'same as everybody else.'"[18] While blacks are often reminded that they are seen as inferior by such treatment as being followed in stores, being quoted higher prices when buying a car, and watching empty cabs pass them by, whites do not receive explicit signs that indicate their privilege. As Paula Rothenberg describes it, white privilege is invisible to most whites.[19] They simply accept such things as shopping in peace, being offered a fair price, and being picked up by a cab as normal. Rather than think themselves advantaged, most whites believe that everyone receives the same opportunities and treatment that they do.

This mindset that white privilege is normal combined with the increasingly pervasive theme of colorblindness in U.S. society makes many whites oblivious to their advantages over blacks. The inability of many whites to recognize their white privilege holds true even for many whites who have close friends who are black. While they may realize that racism exists in society, they are unaware that it results in their having greater privileges than their black friends. Eager to see the common ties that bind them to one another, whites in these friendships are often blind to the disparities between themselves and their friends that are due to racial discrimination.

THE BLACK VIEW

The black interviewees manage to deal with these differences between themselves and their close white friends through a somewhat different strategy. While most are aware that their friends have race-based privileges over them, they distance their friendship from that fact. While U.S. society may be racist and their friends may unavoidably benefit from that racism as a white person, the black interviewees tend to downplay the white privilege of their friends. As noted earlier, they may be well aware that whites are not "the same as everybody else" but, sensing that openly discussing this fact might be harmful to their friendship, they keep this knowledge "on a shelf."

While only thirteen of the white interviewees stated, without prodding, that they had a race-based advantage over their black friends, the overwhelming majority of black interviewees had no trouble discerning their white friend's privilege. Thirty-two of the forty black interviewees maintained that their white friends had an advantage over them as a result of race.[20] Unlike the majority of the white friends, few of the black interviewees hesitated in their answers to that question.

While Ellen's first response to whether racism affects her black friend Pam was "I feel like she's never even thought about it," Pam did not have to be prompted to discuss racism today. As she sees it,

I think that there are some situations that, if I allowed that situation to prevail, that Ellen would be definitely at an advantage. . . . As a society, we've got a long way to go. We've come a long way but we've got a long way to go. And I have to be a realist. Because I know that racism is still alive. And I have to be vigilant. (Pam, black, 50)

While Ellen, like most white people, can avoid racism's interference with her daily life, Pam maintains that she must always be prepared to face it. She stresses, however, that she and Ellen are "not going to allow [racism in society] to become our problem."

Kofi, too, like the majority of the other black interviewees, did not hesitate in answering the question of whether he or his white friend, Dave, has advantages over the other as a result of race.

Well, I think he's advantaged over me due to race. Yah. But, you know, he didn't ask for it. [laughs] He was born and it like just happened. And, yah, I mean, I think so. Because it's the way this society is here. (Kofi, black, 35)

Like Pam, he separates his friend from any negative connotations in his response. Yes, Kofi says, Dave is privileged, but "he didn't ask for it . . . it just happened." When comparing Kofi's and Dave's responses, it is obvious that Kofi has given the issue of racism considerably more thought than Dave. He is quick to say that his white friend has an advantage over him because of race. However, he does not allow that perception to cool his warm feelings toward his friend. Instead, he excuses Dave from any responsibility for that privilege, saying "he didn't ask for it." And they never discuss it.

With different strategies, these two friends have worked together to ensure that race does not come between them. Dave had simply never thought about the issue enough to realize that he had any race-based advantage over Kofi. Kofi, on the other hand, recognizes that Dave has advantages over him as a white man but maintains that "it's just the way society is here" and never brings mention of it into their friendship. He, like most of the other black interviewees, keeps this knowledge "on a shelf" and out of his relationship with his white friend.

While not all the black interviewees stated as explicitly as Kofi their separation of racism in society from their relationship with their white friend, most made comments about their friendship such as "it's not about race" and "it's just personal." In different, yet parallel, ways to the efforts of their white friends, the black friends have managed to place their friendship outside the negativity associated with racial issues in U.S. society. None mentioned having any negative feelings brought on by their white friends having a race-based privilege that they cannot share.

All eight black interviewees who said that their white friends did not have greater race-based privileges than they did were born after the culmination of the civil rights movement, except for Harriet, a fifty-one-year-old. While she first answered, "Yes, as a white woman, yah [Marie Elena] probably has an advantage over me," she began to backtrack, saying that on the other hand, "race might play the other side . . . if someone feels that they would have to do what's politically correct." She went on to say,

I guess I'm kind of waffling because I really never thought about it. She might and she might not. . . . Let's put it this way, it's a possibility she might. But it's a possibility again, depending on the climate. I know she's good at what she does. Anything she gets, she deserves. (Harriet, black, 51)

In just a few sentences, Harriet began to say that whites are privileged in our society and then took back that statement when she began to think of her own friend in light of it.

While one might argue that the other seven black interviewees who do not strongly maintain that their white friend has an advantage over them as a result of race are in denial or simply too young[21] to have experienced the full impact of racism in the United States, Harriet is well versed in racial issues and the history of African Americans. Not only has she taken courses in black studies, she has lived a life embedded in African American history. She grew up in what she describes as "something out of Franklin Frazier's *Black Bourgeoisie*," with national and international figures like Langston Hughes and Oliver Tambo as family friends. Today, Harriet is one of the driving forces behind her church's efforts in dealing with issues of race. She grew up in and has chosen to live today in one of the major black communities in the United States. Racism is an issue that she has grappled with on both a personal and an intellectual level. The fact that she had not thought about her friend's white privilege is a testimony to the power of homophily in friendships.

THE INFLUENCE OF HOMOPHILY ON CLOSE BLACK-WHITE FRIENDSHIPS

As noted in chapter 1, the concept of homophily in friendships, the idea that "like attracts like," combined with the notion that blacks and whites are racial "opposites" has provided a major stumbling block to attempts to understand close black-white friendships. While the results of this study indicate that the concept of homophily should be updated to include the possibility of like being attracted to like across racial lines, it also provides evidence of the continued existence of the racial divide in the United States. These findings make clear, however, the social construction of that separation and the discomfort that even the closest friends of different races have about discussing the reality and ramifications of that divide.

If the friends did openly acknowledge and discuss the differences in privileges that they have as a result of race, they might very likely not see themselves as like one another as they do now. Aside from Hillary, even the white friends who said, without hesitation, that they have an advantage over their black friends rarely, if ever, talk about this fact. These disparities, if recognized, could seriously harm the relationship, as seen in Doris and Hillary's experience described in chapter 3.

This finding supports much of the traditional notion of homophily. Indeed, these results indicate that it is crucial for close friends to believe that they are similar to one another. So much so that many interracial friends will either ignore or avoid focusing on the differences in racial privileges that exist between them. This feat is much easier for the white friends in such pairs than it is for the black ones. As mentioned earlier, in U.S. society where whiteness is seen as the norm, it takes a special effort for whites to recognize white privilege and, in turn, the discrimination faced by blacks. The friends' sense of sameness and the small role that race plays in the friendships has worked to prevent the majority of the white interviewees from noticing their race-based privilege and their black friend's, using Doris's term, "unprivilege." Most blacks, on the other hand, must somehow reconcile the fact that they know that blacks are discriminated against in our society with the fact that one (or more) of their close friends is white.

In many cases, blacks who have close white friends have fewer options when it comes to choosing the race of persons with whom they will become friends. When there is interracial contact that leads to friendship, it most often takes place in a predominantly white setting. All but three of the forty friendships in this sample were formed in settings in which whites were a clear majority. Some of the black interviewees were the only black child in an all-white neighborhood. Others worked in predominantly white settings. For the whites around them, this was a situation in which interracial friendships could develop in a relatively unintimidating environment. They were in the comfortable majority and not facing a large influx of blacks who might challenge their position.

The blacks in this environment, on the other hand, were confronted with the choice of making friends with white people or having few friends or even none at all. If they had any negative racial feelings, it made sense to set them aside as they developed friendships with some of the whites around them. Just as feminist women can find happiness with male friends, in spite of being aware of persistent male domination in society, many blacks have established close friendships with whites even when they acknowledge the racism still in existence throughout the United States. Both blacks and women manage, at least to some degree, to put the racial and sex discrimination they respectively face "on a shelf" when dealing with their friends.[22]

The fact that such interracial friendships do exist, and are becoming more common,[23] reveals that progress has been made in race relations since the civil rights movement. In spite of the institutionalized divisions (such as racial profiling and discrimination in housing and public schooling), that still exist between white and black Americans, the friendship pairs in this sample demonstrate that blacks and whites can, and many indeed do, have much in common with one another. These commonalities, such as economic class, occupation, and the college attended, were much rarer forty years ago.

Moreover, these friendships are affecting the racial views of both the black and white participants. Many whites in these friendships still find it difficult to connect racism in society to their own white privilege in relation to their black friends. However, they all have gained a greater awareness of racial issues in our society. Every interviewee has also become more accepting of members of the other race as a result of their close interracial friendship. While, for the most part, the progress has been in increments and very small steps, all have broadened their perspective on racial issues in the United States.

Chapter 5 focuses on how these close black-white friendships influence the individual friends' perspectives on race and racism. In doing so, it explains that participation in such a friendship increases white awareness of racism in U.S. society and both blacks' and whites' acceptance of members of the other race. It also looks at the number of cross-race friends of each member of the dyad, examining whether someone who develops one interracial friendship is likely to develop several interracial friendships.

NOTES

1. William Julius Wilson, *The Declining Significance of Race* (Chicago: University of Chicago Press, 1978).

2. William Julius Wilson, "Affirming Opportunity," *American Prospect* 10, 46 (Sept.–Oct. 1999). Accessed at http://www.prospect.org/print/V10/46/wilson-w.html.

3. Gallup Organization. "Special Reports: Black–White Relations in the United States, 2001 Update." July 10, 2001. Accessed at http://www.gallup.com/poll/reports/bwr2001/sr010711.asp.

4. One of the three maintained that the discrimination blacks face and their experiences as a numerical minority that must deal with people of another race is actually an advantage because it makes them stronger. The other two both described facing racial discrimination as they grew up but still said that whites and blacks have relatively equal opportunities today.

5. Of course, there are always exceptions to this rule. For instance, in two of the forty pairs of interviewees both friends maintain that they are "very" different from each other. They recognize these dissimilarities and often marvel at how much they like each other despite these differences.

6. Erving Goffman, *Interaction Ritual* (New York: Doubleday, 1967).

7. Erving Goffman, *The Presentation of Self in Everyday Life* (Garden City, NY: Doubleday, 1959).

8. Paula Rothenberg, *Invisible Privilege: A Memoir About Race, Class, and Gender* (Lawrence: University Press of Kansas, 2000).

9. Ibid.

10. Ruth Frankenberg, *White Women, Race Matters: The Social Construction of Whiteness* (Minneapolis: University of Minnesota Press, 1993).

11. See Manning Marable, *Black Leadership* (New York: Columbia University Press, 1998), p. 153.

12. Joe Feagin and Hernán Vera, *White Racism* (New York: Routledge, 1995), p. 14.

13. In fact, the mere mention of the phrase *affirmative action* increases the antipathy of both liberal and conservative whites towards blacks. See "The Hidden Truth About Liberals and Affirmative Action" by Richard Morin, *The Washington Post*, Sunday, Sept. 21, 1997; Page C05.

14. The other one immediately brought up her experience with what she described as "reverse discrimination," when answering the question on possible advantages she or her black friend have over the other as a result of race. After describing how she was denied a job offer because of an affirmative-action program, her initial answer to the question was that she did not believe that she had any advantages over her friend. She

eventually reluctantly stated that she "guess[es] there is some disadvantage" to be being black.

15. A look at what major Internet search engines and directories such as Google and Yahoo turn up when searching for "reverse racism" provides evidence of this point.

16. Poll results on affirmative action have been known to vary dramatically from the wording of the question. The 2001 Gallup poll question on affirmative action was phrased as follows: "In general, do you think we need to increase, keep the same, or decrease affirmative-action programs in this country?" See Gallup, "Special Reports."

17. Ashley W. Doane Jr., "Dominant Group Ethnic Identity in the United States," *Sociological Quarterly* 38, 3 (Summer 1997): 379.

18. Doane, "Dominant Group."

19. Rothenberg, *Invisible Privilege.*

20. One of the remaining eight, Joe, an eighteen-year-old college student, said that the harassment that he has faced because of his race (e.g., being stopped by a New Jersey state trooper practicing racial profiling) actually gives him an advantage over Devin, his white friend. He maintained that having to deal with such things makes him a stronger person. Another of the five acknowledged that racism exists in society but stated that she has not faced it often personally and does not believe that her friend has any race-based advantages over her. One other interviewee said that she is "proper enough to hold her own" in a white setting and that her white friend has received more flak spending time amidst blacks than she, herself, has among whites.

21. Five of the others are college student in their late teens and early twenties. Four of the seven actually said that that may be in denial, stating that they "don't like to think" about issues of racism or that they are "in a bubble." One, Liz, is a thirty-four-year-old who, while maintaining that her white friend does not have any race-based advantages over her, believes that racism does exist in U.S. society. She said that she thinks she has been spared the brunt of it because of her nonthreatening, petite figure.

22. Of course, black females must deal with "double oppression."

23. See chapter 1.

5

New Perspectives on Race

I used to think that just because someone had a different color skin, they were, you know, that they were like a criminal or whatever. . . . And then [after becoming close friends with Joe] it was like, "What was I thinking? What was wrong with me?" You know? It's like—it's really, it's definitely a positive thing for me—definitely. And it has influenced my opinions of other people. . . . Now I look at, like, a black and a white that aren't getting along and say, "What's your problem?" It's kind of flipped over.

Devin, white, 19

It showed me that just because I come across some white people that don't like black people—or some white people that feel like we're inferior to them—does not mean that everyone white is like . . . that.

Latrice, black, 18

In our racially stratified society, most people view members of other races from across a racial divide. They form their attitudes toward members of different races while ensconced among their own racial group. In these environments, racial stereotypes often flourish uninhibited. On the other hand, participants in cross-race friendships have a relatively unique up-close view of members of other races. This perspective often enables them to see through racial myths and gain insights into racial issues more easily than those who remain only on one side of the racial divide. This chapter examines the new perspectives on race that blacks and whites gain from their experiences in a close cross-racial friendship.

The racial divide between whites and blacks would be notably wider without the influence of the cross-race friendships that now exist. These friendships effectively negate stereotypes and tighten the bonds between Americans of "opposite" races. All of the white and the black interviewees maintained that their close interracial friendships influenced their perspective on race. While most of the white interviewees maintained that their close friendships with a black person taught them to view other blacks as "potential friends," many of the black interviewees said that their close cross-racial friendships enabled them to realize that not all white people are "mean."

All the interviewees were asked a series of questions about their childhood experiences with racial issues. Most of the friends in this sample were the first in their immediate families to cross the racial divide. Only thirteen[1] black and two white interviewees said that their parents formed close interracial friends before them (see Table 5.1). The majority of the interviewees grew up in households who never felt the presence of a member of the other race.

Almost half of the white interviewees said that race was never discussed in their families as they grew up (see Table 5.2). It was simply not an issue for them. They grew up in predominantly white communities and hardly, if ever, interacted across racial lines. For these interviewees, whiteness was simply seen as "normal."[2] No blacks came over to their homes and few, if any, lived nearby or attended the same classes in school.[3] These interviewees did not recall serious household discussions of even national race-related news events, such as the Los Angeles riots in 1992, when many of the younger interviewees still lived with their families of origin.

Only 10 percent of the white friends maintained that race was given much notice in their households (see Table 5.2). Two of these four interviewees described having serious discussions with their parents in which blacks were portrayed in a generally positive light.[4] The other two interviewees recalled growing up in households where racist thoughts were voiced openly and often by their parents. All four of these interviewees grew up before or during the civil

Table 5.1
Cross-Racial Friendships of Parents of Interviewees*

	Parents had Cross-Racial Friendships	Parents Did Not Have Cross-Racial Friendships
Black interviewees	13	26
White interviewees	2	38

*White adoptive parents of one interviewee not included.

Table 5.2
White Families of Origin and Discussions About Race

Race was seriously discussed with blacks viewed positively	2
Race was not discussed	16
Race was brought up only fleetingly through racist comments	20
Race was seriously discussed with blacks viewed negatively	2

rights movement. Most of the white interviewees who maintained that their families of origin discussed racism said they did so only fleetingly when a family member would make a racist comment.

On the other hand, almost 75 percent of the black interviewees said that their parents often discussed racial issues with them. All but three[5] of the eighteen black interviewees over thirty recalled warnings from a parental figure about the dangers of living in a society where racism is prevalent. Most described parental instructions that they had to be "twice as good" as whites if they were to succeed in life.

Crossing the racial divide affects both blacks and whites, but somewhat differently because of their distinct experiences with race. As noted in previous chapters, whites do not generally feel pressure to understand the cultures of people of color or recognize white privilege. They have no need to learn a culture or perspective other than their own to advance in U.S. society. For most whites, their close friendship with a black person is their first sustained interaction with someone of a different culture or perspective on race. Blacks, on the other hand, must understand how to interact with white people in order to advance in mainstream society. As W. E. B. Du Bois describes it, they must have a "double consciousness" and learn to live in two worlds.[6] Although many learn to succeed in predominantly white work environments, most never socialize with their white colleagues after hours. For both blacks and whites, interacial friendships open a door to a deeper understanding of the other race than they could ever attain through simply work-related relationships.

EFFECTS ON WHITE FRIENDS

All the white interviewees maintained that their close interracial friendships affected their views on race. Even the few white interviewees who initially believed that their close friendship with a black person did not influence their views on race concluded, after further thought, that the friendship did have such an impact. For example, Beth, a fifty-year-old who only reluctantly stated that whites may have more race-based privileges than blacks, at first denied that her almost decade-long friendship with Sandra had influenced her perspective on racial issues. When asked whether she thinks her friendship with Sandra has affected how she views race or issues of race, Beth responded:

Not really because of. I've never been prejudiced. I don't think I've ever been prejudiced or bigoted. I think I just try to respect the dignity of human beings regardless of the color. But maybe it's made me a little bit more aware of some things . . .—you know, for example, on a couple of occasions.—and very infrequently has this happened—we might go somewhere and—she has said this happened to her all the time—go to a cleaners and there'd be a line of people there and they'd wait on all the other colors first, before her, and just not treat her with respect. And maybe once or twice we were somewhere and waiting and they really should have, maybe, tended to her first and didn't. [She says] that happens a lot. So, maybe I would be a little more sensitive to that. (Beth, white, 50)

While Beth maintains that she's "never been prejudiced or bigoted" herself, her friendship with Sandra has increased her awareness of racial bigotry in the United States.

Carl believes that his friendship with Charles, his black college roommate, has deepened his conviction of the innate equality between blacks and whites. When asked whether his friendship with Charles has influenced his views on race, he, like Beth, initially denied its effects.

Probably not really. . . . I mean, I would never have a thought in my mind to question anybody of a different race or anything like that. But before [having Charles as my roommate], I never really had any, I never really had the proof to not . . . make an assumption of somebody. But now I have the proof. So, therefore, I don't have to worry about it. (Carl, white, 18)

Now that he has become close friends with Charles, Carl can safely dismiss any nagging stereotypes he may have had about blacks. Carl now has the "proof" that he should not make "assumptions" about members of other races. Implied in his answer is the notion that without the personal interracial interaction in this friendship, Carl would at least partially believe racial stereotypes.

Kyle, now twenty-three and friends with Patrick since childhood, echoed Carl's thoughts when reflecting on how his friendship with Patrick has influenced his views on race.

Even if I didn't know Patrick, I might still. I think I'd still have the same views as I do towards [race]. But it just makes you, you know, it just makes you, fortifies that, you know, that people are people, regardless of race or color. . . . I guess that's what I've learned, like, you base people, you know, on one-on-one. You don't base them because of, you know, what they look like or their beliefs or something. Yah, I would think like being friends with him just, you know, it just like cemented those views. (Kyle, white, 23)

Like Beth and Carl, Kyle believes that his close friendship with a black person has simply confirmed the colorblind beliefs that he already had.

One white interviewee maintained that he had previous racist beliefs that his close interracial friendship changed. Devin described how his friendship with Joe dramatically altered how he views blacks and race relations in general.

I think [my friendship with Joe has influenced my views on race], actually. It's strange because, at first, when we first started becoming really good friends, I didn't think of it, like, as anything. And then, as we've become so close, it's been kind of like a, it's like, you know. I used to think that just because someone had a different color skin, they were, you know, that they were like a criminal or whatever. I really didn't think it too harshly, but it was just kind of like the stereotype. And then it was like, "What was I thinking? What was wrong with me?" You know? It's like, . . . it's really, it's definitely a positive thing for me—definitely. And it has influenced my opinions of other people. . . . Now I look at . . . like a black and a white that aren't getting along and say, "What's your problem?" It's kind of flipped over. (Devin, white, 19)

After crossing the racial divide himself, Devin's perspective on race is so altered he is now angered by the prejudice he observes. Instead of picturing a criminal when he looks at a black person, he now thinks of his friend Joe. In Carl's words, he now has "proof" that overpowers the stereotype that all black men are criminals.

While Devin admitted that he once saw blacks as criminals, most white interviewees simply maintain that, before their initial close friendship with a black person, they never viewed blacks as potential friends. Consistent with the traditional understandings of race and homophily discussed in earlier chapters, they viewed blacks as racial opposites with whom they would have little, if anything, in common. Cindy, a twenty-year-old college student, is representative of many white interviewees. She described how her friendship with Kia has influenced her view of race.

[At] my school, and the way we always grew up . . . everybody kind of sat together by race. . . . [But] now, since I know that I am such good friends with Kia, I know that I could become good friends with other minorities as well. And so, I look for those friendships more and consider them potential friendships rather than just someone who, like, who wouldn't mix or talk. (Cindy, white, 20)

Cindy might not have viewed all black people as bad before she became friends with Kia, but she certainly did not perceive them as potential friends.

Patricia, a sixty-five–year-old white interviewee, was forty-eight before she began to work closely with some black people and had her first opportunity to become friends with a black person.

Maybe this has been such a unique experience for me because I never had [a black friend] before and so it makes me feel good. I feel like I've come a long way, baby. . . . And I, I just feel fortunate. I just think it's unfortunate that other people, you know, that other people can't experience this. . . . It makes people more understanding. That's what's made me more understanding. (Patricia, white, 65)

Like the other white interviewees, Cindy and Patricia altered their perspectives on race after establishing close interracial friendships. They have come a long way in their perspectives on racial issues and black Americans. Whereas whites tend to see blacks as a monolithic "other" before their friendships, they gain a clearer picture of blacks as individuals once they have a close black friend.

WHITE FRIENDS WHO ACTIVELY FIGHT RACISM

For some whites, this clearer picture motivates them to actively fight racism. As demonstrated in chapter 4, many white friends now stress the individuality of their friends so much they lose sight of their friends' race. However, some whites are able to remain aware of both the differences in race-based privileges and the commonalities that exist between themselves and their black friends. This knowledge that their friends, who are often like them in many ways, face racial discrimination in our society gives them a sense of obligation to fight for racial justice. Eleven of the forty white interviewees spoke of actively working against racism. These friends mentioned specific ways that they actively contest racism, such as speaking out at antiracism rallies on campus, joining antiracist organizations, making a conscious effort to promote interracial dialogue at work, and joining protest marches against racism. Six indicated that it was their close friendship with a black person that was one of the primary sparks that helped ignite their commitment to fight racial discrimination.[7]

Eileen O'Brien, in *Whites Confront Racism*, describes such an impetus for antiracism work as "borrowed approximations."[8] Among O'Brien's sample of white antiracists, the most common explanation for why they became active in antiracist work was having witnessed racial oppression. Most often, this entailed seeing a black friend or acquaintance confronted with racial discrimination. In some cases, one can be driven to act against racism simply by having read accounts or seeing media portrayals of racism. In this sample of forty close black-white friends, the majority of whites who actively fight racism point to the knowledge of the racism their friends face as the catalyst behind their antiracism activity.

Barbara, an eighty-four-year-old woman from the Midwest, was the only white interviewee who indicated that any of her white friends openly disapproved of her having black friends. However, she did not let this criticism stop her from developing many close friendships with black people as her neighborhood and church changed racially. Before moving into a neighborhood that was widely perceived to be vulnerable to redlining,[9] Barbara had never personally interacted with black people. However, once her neighborhood and church, as many predicted, began to "darken," Barbara embraced her new neighbors and fellow parishioners. This decision to remain when the racial dividing line approached and then swept past her brought her both joy from new friendships and tensions within old ones.

[My close friendships with blacks have given] me a lot of problems because my white friends [have] not [been] open to this at all. . . . I know . . . people kind of would see me have someone black—maybe Lil—over. And ah. It really was. You know, they just didn't like it very well, I don't think. But they didn't understand it. And I don't think they do any better [now] but they know that's how it is in the real world. And I don't think I've contributed a lot to the world but I do think that, you know, some of my white friends know that I have good black friends. (Barbara, white, 84)

Now that Barbara has crossed the racial divide, she feels obliged not only to lead by quiet example, but also to respond to racism where she sees it. She described having to "almost throttle somebody the other night" for making racist remarks during dinner at the elder living complex to which she recently moved.

Evan has now come to the point where he makes efforts to not only cross the racial divide himself but to also bring others across. For instance, he speaks to blacks in situations where little interracial interaction is occurring in an attempt to diminish stereotypes that both whites and blacks may have of the other race.

I can tell you I've been in situations where I have consciously made an effort. Like there was a company-sponsored party and I remember that all the African Americans sat together in one area. And I made a conscious effort to go over there and sit there myself. . . . There were a lot of other white people around. They congregated together. Black people all congregated together. And I sat with the black people just because I felt like there needed to be a presence there, among other things. Just, someone's got to do it, is the way I felt. I still was uncomfortable.

When asked what made him feel he was the person to do it, Evan replied:

A sense of obligation, I guess. . . . Just an understanding that if you don't do anything it won't get better. I mean, regardless, I guess that's what draws me. I feel that sense of obligation. If you don't do it, it won't get better. And I know from my own life that so often I've judged people by their appearances and found that to be completely wrong about them. (Evan, white, 41)

Evan's friendship with Bob, a man whom he initially saw as a "swinging, wise, you know, black male—with an attitude" enabled him to realize how stereotypes once influenced his impression of blacks. He now actively works on dismantling his own stereotypes and helping others see past theirs.

Carol's description of how she feels when surrounded by only white people is similar to that of many black interviewees. Carol has educated herself about the racial discrimination in U.S. society and feels so committed to racial justice that she feels burdened when around white people who are unaware of racial realities.

Once you see what black folks see, you become more comfortable with black folks in certain situations than you do with white folks. You know, you can talk about things that you really don't have to explain. You know, where with white folks, you're *always* unpacking and *always* unpacking and always unpacking, you know. So . . . I don't feel comfortable in an all-white group. It's just not my reality anymore. I need diversity. I just need it. I couldn't, you know. There are places in this country where I wouldn't go if I was called [to minister]. 'Cause I just can't. Oh, well, let's not get into that. If God wanted me to live in that misery. . . . But you *know* I would be working on it! You know, if He put me there, it would be for a reason. [laughs] I couldn't leave it behind. See, that's the burden of it. You know. I can't live as if I don't know what I know. (Carol, white, 57)

Carol, like slightly more than one-fourth of the white interviewees, feels obliged to use her new perspective on race to improve race relations in society.

As noted earlier, all the white interviewees maintain that their interracial friendships have widened their views on racial issues in the United States. Having crossed the racial divide, they now see race from a different perspective. All spoke with appreciation of feeling closely connected to a member of the "opposite" race. Many described themselves as lucky or even blessed to have such a friendship.

However, the effects of close interracial friendships are different for those white friends who now actively combat racism and those who do not. The interviewees who feel obliged to fight racism spoke of the burdens as well as the blessings that can come with the knowledge one gains from crossing the divide. They have become quite aware of their own white privilege and the racial discrimination that their friends must face as black persons in the United States. Unlike the majority of the white friends, who tend to ignore or push aside the racial differences between themselves and their friends, ten of the eleven[10] white friends who actively fight racism are very cognizant of the disparities that accompany these differences in a racist society. While they do not talk about race constantly with their black friends, they do, on occasion, have serious discussions on racial issues. They are interested in learning their black friends' perspective on race and expanding their own. Moreover, they feel an impetus to act on this knowledge, even though it is not always easy for them to do so. Eileen O'Brien points out that this can be "both . . . unpopular and unsafe."[11] As Carol describes it, "the burden of seeing [racism and white privilege] is that you have to keep talking about what you see" in a society where most people do not want to hear it.

These white people who have crossed the racial divide and made connections between societal racism and the experiences of their black friends are similar to Robert Park's "marginal men," who are destined to live as strangers in two "different" and "antagonistic" cultures.[12] While not "of" the black community, whites who recognize racial discrimination and white privilege are different from most members of the white community. Like Park's "marginal men," they now have a wider horizon in their perspectives on racial issues than those who have not crossed the racial divide. The perspective they have on race relations is different from that of most white people. Most whites never personally interact with blacks and even most of those who do so do not make the connection between their friends' experiences and racism in society. Like "marginal men," those who do make those links can never again have a sense of complete belonging among whites who are unaware of their racial privilege.

While nine of the nineteen white friends over the age of thirty discussed efforts they have made to fight racial discrimination, very few of the younger white interviewees said that they actively work to alleviate racism in U.S. society. Only two of the twenty-one interviewees under thirty described seeking out ways to improve race relations between whites and blacks. These results echo those found by Mary Jackman and Marie Crane in their article " 'Some of My Best Friends Are Black . . .': Interracial Friendships and White Racial

Attitudes."[13] Jackman and Crane found that the effects of having black friends and acquaintances were much more likely to affect whites' affection toward blacks and belief in stereotypes about blacks than it was to affect their public policy views. In other words, most whites who interact on a friendly basis with blacks do not feel any personal animosity toward blacks, but neither will they vote for policies that promote equality between the racial groups. According to Jackman and Crane, whites, as a group, are very reluctant to relinquish the inequality from which they benefit—even if they do view blacks as potential friends.

Most of the younger adults in the sample are in college environments and just beginning to form a sense of how individuals may affect society. The increasing popularity of the colorblind perspective on race no doubt has also heavily influenced younger white Americans and made it especially difficult for them to perceive their race-based privilege. However, even the white interviewees who do not actively fight racism articulated some degree of change in their perspective on race through their close interracial friendships. Like the majority of the respondents in Jackman and Crane's study, they are less likely to see blacks as stereotypical figures and more likely to view them as potential friends.

EFFECTS ON BLACK FRIENDS

As noted earlier, W. E. B. Du Bois described black Americans as possessing a "double-consciousness,"[14] from living in both a black and a white world. This notion might lead one to expect that blacks are already interacting relatively comfortably with whites and have less to learn from close interracial friendships than do whites. None of the black interviewees maintained that they learned about white privilege or racial discrimination from their white friends. All thirty-seven who believe that whites have greater privileges than blacks in U.S. society developed this point of view before they ever had a close white friend. However, all the black friends maintained that their interracial friendships have influenced how they view race and racial issues. As with the effects of close interracial friendships on whites, the influence of such friendships on blacks' views on racial issues ranged from the modest to the intense.

Many black interviewees overcame negative stereotypes of white people through their close friendships. For example, Yvette says that growing up in a predominantly white neighborhood and having close friendships with whites taught her to choose her friends by their personalities rather than their race.

Well, it's just taught me that there's good and bad in both sides. That's what I've learned. There's good and bad in both sides. And that's why you just choose your friends on who you get along with. (Yvette, black, 39)

Yvette recognizes friendship potential within both races, a common phenomenon among both the black and the white friends.

A significant minority of the black friends said their perception of whites changed dramatically because of their interracial friendships. One-fourth maintained that their interracial relationships revealed to them that not all white people are racist. Patrick described how this occurred in his own life.

I used to kind of think a lot of white people were mean. And even if they showed a little bit of niceness towards you, overall, I [thought] white people were kind of all pretty racist. But Kyle showed me that there's some really good [white] people out there. (Patrick, black, 23)

Having experienced racial taunts and the disappointment of fair-weather friends in his white neighborhood, Patrick had begun to form a negative view of all whites before he became friends with Kyle.

Many of the black interviewees spoke of overcoming negative impressions of white people through the interracial friendships they formed as adults. As described in chapter 3, almost all the black interviewees reported facing racial discrimination from whites. Many described their close interracial friendships as offering their first experience of the potential goodness in white people (see Table 5.3). Latrice's description of the effects of her close interracial friendship is typical among these friends.

It showed me that just because I come across some white people that don't like black people—or some white people that feel like we're inferior to them—does not mean that . . . every white person is like that. (Latrice, black, 18)

The fact that, as noted in chapter 1, only 15 percent of blacks have a close white friend[15] is particularly sobering in light of such statements by Latrice and one-fourth of the other black interviewees.

Pam, raised in an all-black neighborhood in the Deep South before the civil rights movement, lived through a period when Jim Crow laws were still enforced. She believes that her experiences of friendships with whites and moving to racially diverse areas enabled her to be more accepting of whites as individuals than her family members who remained in their still all-black neighborhood.

Table 5.3
Black Families of Origin and Discussions About Race by Age*

	Had Discussions About Race	Did Not Have Discussions About Race
Under 30	12[+]	8
30 or older	15	3

*Interviewees raised outside United States not included (N = 2).
[+]White adoptive family (N = 1) included: racial issues discussed "not often."

I think I'm able to have a broader view [than my family who remained at home]. I think my attitudes are different because I've been exposed to a lot of different . . . kinds of people. . . . I'm more accepting of other people than my siblings and my mother. (Pam, black, 53)

Her words are echoed by Chris, a black interviewee who grew up in an all-black neighborhood three decades after Pam. Reflecting on his friendship with his white friend, Matt, Chris explains that

It's like real important that you get to know, like, say other races. And it's real important to, like, even become friends, like real *good* friends with other races. . . . It's just like a different feeling—a new feeling. You know, and you *will* learn a lot. Trust me. You learn a lot. (Chris, black, 19)

Chris says that he has learned a lot through his friendship with Matt that has made him more open-minded toward whites.

Like Chris, Vanessa realized that her view of white people was tinged by stereotypes before she developed her own close friendships with whites at college. Her friendship with Mary Anne, her white roommate, and Mary Anne's white friends

changed my views a lot. I mean I see them. I've always seen them, like, in the same light as others but I actually understand more. I can see where they're coming from and why people act the way they do. . . . Like even with myself. I caught myself judging a book by its cover. Seeing them as like these Valley High girls, you know, that just don't do anything but go to the mall and just spend money, borrow Daddy's checkbook, take his credit card, okay? You know, and I've seen them for who they are and I think they see me for who I am also. And that respect is there. (Vanessa, black, 18)

If Vanessa and Mary Anne had not been assigned together as roommates, it is likely that both of them would still be viewing blacks and whites through the stereotypical views they held before they knew one another. Neither thinks they ever would have become friends if they had not been brought together as roommates.

Many of the black interviewees described the professional, as well as the personal, benefits they believe that they have attained through their interracial friendships. For instance James, a college student, said:

If I didn't have diverse friends when I was younger and to this day, like, I'd probably be like not as open to it, y'know. So, being that I've grown up with it, it allows me to be able to socialize with people of all races now. Which is going to help me later on when I'm in the business world or something, y'know. Being able to socialize with all types of people, y'know. You can relate to them better if you know something. But if you don't, you're just like, there's nothing to say. (James, black, 18)

Proponents of affirmative action programs in colleges and universities often defend such efforts on the basis of their beneficial effects on *white* students who will have to operate in an increasingly diverse workforce.[16] Yet many of the black interviewees in this sample are very aware of the professional edge they have gained through exposure to members of other races. The black friends noted this benefit of their cross-racial friendships far more often than did the white interviewees.

Tracy, now a professor, describes how her friendships with whites have enabled her to feel more confident around white colleagues.

I was just thinking about this today because a white friend of mine invited my seminary to take part in this seminar with the rest of the faculty. And I was thinking, you know, I'm not afraid of white people. I don't think white people are—I know that white people aren't better than black people. [laughs] And I know that from *years* of experience. And I know that white people aren't smarter than black people. I know that white people are people. . . . It's kind of like it's debunked whatever kinds of myths I might have had or that [are] easy to have in this society about the other race. (Tracy, black, 50)

Having been told throughout her childhood that she had to work hard to be "better" than whites, Tracy once interpreted this message to mean that whites were innately superior. It took years of close interactions with whites for her to realize that, while the deck may be stacked in favor of whites, they are fundamentally no better than she is.

Bob makes the point that it is possible to work alongside people for years and not really get to know them.

Well, I think that you have to have a relationship with people to really understand them. I think more than change, I think [my friendship with Evan has] matured my view about race relations. . . . I don't look at my white associates as all being the same, somebody you can't trust, somebody that doesn't care about you, somebody that you can't enjoy spending time with, that has [no] common interests that you have. . . . I think my relationship with Evan has kind of helped me to mature to that level of thinking. (Bob, black, 43)

While Bob had worked with many white people, he never viewed them as people with whom he might have interests in common or as potential friends until his close friendship with Evan.

Bob's close friendship with a white person enabled him to have a different, clearer perspective of members of the other race. As in the experience of the white interviewees, black interviewees found stereotypes about the other race debunked through their close interracial friendships. Moreover, all the interviewees now see other members of the "opposite" race as potential friends.

DO THESE FRIENDSHIPS LEAD TO FURTHER INTERRACIAL FRIENDSHIPS?

As noted earlier, approximately three-fourths of the friends in this sample were the first in their immediate families to establish close interracial friendships. It is unclear, however, how many people will follow their example or even how many other cross-racial friends they themselves will make. More of the black friends than white friends reported multiple cross-racial friendships. Reflecting the relatively white environments that they live and work in, slightly over half the black interviewees have a somewhat even balance of white and black friends (18) or almost all white (6) or all white (1) friends. The remaining fifteen black friends live among and interact socially, aside from their one close white friend, almost exclusively with other blacks (see Table 5.4).[17]

While thirteen of the white interviewees socialize with a mixture of whites and blacks and two interact primarily with black people, almost three-fourths of the whites in the sample have only one or few black friends (see Table 5.5).

As noted in chapter 2 most interracial friendships develop in predominantly white environments because of racial segregation in the United States. The few blacks in these arenas are more likely to have interracial friends than are their white friends, who have far more same race peers around them. Likewise, blacks who live in predominantly black settings are less apt to make white friends than those who live in mixed or predominantly white settings.

This influence of segregation on friendship formation is evident in the racial makeup of the friends of the parents of the younger interviewees (see Table 5.6). All six of the interviewees under thirty who grew up in predominantly poor black areas had parents who socialized primarily with blacks. Among the eleven younger interviewees raised in almost-all-white middle-class neighborhoods, only three had parents who interacted primarily with blacks. The parents of the other eight had close interracial friendships.

Table 5.4
Cross-Racial Friendships Among the Black Friends

Only one white friend	7
Primarily black friends	8
Relatively even number of whites and blacks among friends	18
Primarily white friends	6
All white friends	1

Table 5.5
Cross-Racial Friendships Among the White Friends

Only one black friend	14
Primarily white friends	11
Relatively even number of whites and blacks among friends	13
Primarily black friends	2

Table 5.6
Cross-Racial Friendships of Younger Black Interviewee's Parents* by Economic Class and Racial Makeup of Neighborhood

	All Black	Mixture of Races
Poor/primarily black neighborhood	6	0
Middle to upper-middle/primarily white	3	8

*Numbers exclude two interviewees raised abroad, one black child of adoptive white parents, one who came to the United States as a child but whose parents still live in Africa, and one who has a white mother.

Two of the three who grew up in largely white areas but whose parents interacted primarily with blacks said that their parents voiced misgivings about their children's friendships with whites.[18] In both cases, the parents feared that their children were becoming too "white" and losing their sense of identity as black people. This produced tension in both households. For instance, Maria's mother complained when her friends, reflecting the neighborhood, were primarily white.

My mom, she would get really mad at me for stupid things. And, like, we had a lot of arguments. . . . It would kind of turn into this whole thing, well, you know, my daughter's acting really white. I need to expose her to, to other kids just like her. I really don't want her to act like the kids in this town. And she would have like little arguments with me about stuff like that. . . . She thought I was acting quote prissy or I was learning too many things from my friends and I needed to hang out with other kids like me and just stupidness. (Maria, black, 20)

Maria's mother has not altered her views on the subject of her daughter's friends. Steven, however, the other black interviewee who dealt with parental disapproval of his white friends, believes that he has changed his mother's perspective and that she now feels more comfortable with the knowledge that he has predominantly white friends. She now "realizes that, you know, this is the situation that I'm in. And that, you know, I'm not unhappy in it. You know, I'm actually very happy with my friends and my life." He thinks that, under his influence, she is now more open to interracial friendships and increasingly socializes with white coworkers.

Four of the parents of the eleven black interviewees under thirty who resided in predominantly white middle- or upper-middle-class neighborhoods and had a racial mixture of friends themselves rarely talked about race with their children. Just as many middle-class parents of biracial children born after the civil rights movement rarely spoke with their offspring about race,[19] neither did these black parents who raised their children in primarily white environments. According to the interviewees, the only times discussions of race arose revolved around incidents of racism the children confronted. On such occasions, the parents most often advised their children to ignore the racist behavior of others. In both cases, it appears that the parents espoused colorblindness and behaved as if race did not matter.

Three out of these four interviewees were the only three black friends, out of the entire sample of forty, who maintained that whites are not advantaged from racial discrimination in U.S. society.[20] These interviewees are unique in that their parents raised them across the racial divide yet acted, in as many ways as possible, as if the divide did not exist. However, as mentioned previously, even these black interviewees, whose parents had white friends and worked hard to ignore racial divisions in society, reported experiences of racial discrimination. Even as they stated that blacks and whites have relatively equal privileges in our society, their stories of racial discrimination indicated that they had experienced effects of the racial divide.

Cross-racial friendships do much to mitigate the divide. For all the members of these forty close black-white friendships, the racial divide has diminished and become less of a barrier to further interracial friendships. All the white friends maintain that they have an improved perspective on race and racial issues. Six[21] of the eleven whites in the sample who proactively fight racism say that their cross-racial friendships were the initial impetus that led them to actively work to improve race relations.

Each of the black interviewees also maintains that his or her close interracial friendship has positively influenced his or her perspective on race. One-fourth of the black interviewees stated that their friendship with a white person enabled them to perceive that some whites are decent and can be trusted. Another fourth of the black friends reported feeling advantaged over others in the workforce who do not have such friendships, and those interviewees also reported a relatively high comfort level around members of other races.

However beneficial these friendships are to black–white relations, they depend on an environment that will foster them. Just as close cross-racial friendships have the potential to improve race relations, as well as positively affect individual lives, the solutions to the separation that now exists between most blacks and whites must be structurally as well as personally grounded. Chapter 6 focuses on the potential influence of black-white friendships on U.S. society and suggests ways to create environments more conducive to such friendships.

NOTES

1. Another interviewee, Harriet, said that her parents closely interacted with some white people who had married into the family and socialized themselves primarily in the black community.

2. See chapter 4 for a further discussion of whiteness as "normal."

3. Only two grew up having much interaction with blacks. One was raised in a neighborhood that transitioned from white to black during her youth. The other

interviewee's father was a high school coach who often brought his predominantly black teams over to the house.

4. The two interviewees described these conversations as, respectively, about the civil rights movement and the innate equality of all people, no matter what their color.

5. One, Lil, says that while race was not spoken of much in her childhood home, it was simply "understood" that she and her siblings would stay away from the white parts of town.

6. W. E. B. Du Bois, *The Souls of Black Folk: Essays and Sketches* (Greenwich, CT: Fawcett, 1961).

7. Among these six, four said that their cross-racial friendships were *the* spark that led to their antiracist activism, one indicated that his faith-driven antiracism and his cross-racial friendship arose simultaneously, and one said that she already practiced antiracism but that her cross-racial friendship allowed her to go deeper into antiracism work. The other five of the eleven indicated that they had a commitment to such work even before having developed a close friendship with a black person. They revealed that their sense of obligation to do such work is faith-driven.

8. Eileen O'Brien, *Whites Confront Racism: Antiracists and Their Paths to Action* (New York: Rowman & Littlefield, 2001).

9. As Barbara described it, shortly after she and her husband bought their house, the only people who were allowed to buy into the neighborhood were blacks. Mortgage lenders and real-estate agents worked together to ensure that the blacks who wished to buy homes in that city were steered toward her neighborhood.

10. The eleventh, a college student, has not at this point made the connection between personal prejudice and structural discrimination.

11. O'Brien, *When Whites Confront Racism*, p. 17.

12. Robert Park, Introduction to *The Marginal Man*, by Everett V. Stonequist (New York: Russell & Russell, 1937).

13. Mary R. Jackman and Marie Crane, "'Some of My Best Friends Are Black . . .': Interracial Friendship and Whites' Racial Attitudes," *Public Opinion Quarterly* 50, 4 (1986): 459–86.

14. Du Bois, *Souls of Black Folk*, p. 12.

15. Jennifer Lach, "Interracial Friendships Slip?" *American Demographics* 00 (Jan. 2000). Accessed at http://www.inside.com/product/Product.asp?pf_id = {6A9B44F8-A949-49EE-8468-FCA343538E93}.

16. See, for example, "The Diversity Dilemma." *Commonweal*, March 9, 2001, pp. 5, 6, and the expert report of Patricia Gurin in *Gratz et al. v. Bollinger et al.* and in *Grutter et al. v. Bollinger et al.* Accessed at www.umich.edu/~urel/admissions/legal /expert/gurintoc.html.

17. The remaining five are two international college students who grew up outside the United States, an interviewee who came to the United States as a boy but whose parents reside in Africa, the interviewee with a white mother, and the interviewee adopted by white parents.

18. Rod was the only black interviewee over thirty who also discussed facing such pressure. His father, an activist in the civil rights movement, repeatedly complained that Rod did not have enough black friends. Rod, in turn, grew frustrated at his father's complaints, pointing out that it was his parents who decided that he should go to a virtually all-white prep school.

19. For an in-depth discussion of this, see my book *From Black to Biracial* (Westport, CT: Praeger, 1999).

20. The fourth, who expressed the belief that whites do have greater than privileges than blacks, is almost thirty and has approximately a decade more life experience than the other three.

21. Again, two of these six said that their faith and their interracial friendships were contemporaneous impetuses for their antiracist efforts.

6

Bridging the Institutionalized Racial Divide

In my freshman year of high school is when the schools integrated. I remember that very well. . . . But most of the kids at that time, even though we were integrated, most of the white kids moved away. So, even though it was a mixed school, there were very few white people still at [my] high school when I was growing up. So, it wasn't until I started work at [a relatively diverse organization] that I feel like I grew up and to realize that people were all the same. You know, one person's not any better than the other when it comes to [race].

Lil, black, 59

The neighborhood we've been living in for like seventeen years is very racially mixed. And, to me, that's always been a good thing. . . . [I wanted my kids] to be more aware of other cultures than I was when I grew up and I think there's an enriching experience in that.

Jan, white, 50

As indicated in chapter 5, individual racism can be effectively reduced when blacks and whites interact as peers and form friendships. However, institutional racism often prevents such interactions from ever taking place. While individual racism takes place by the active efforts of one or more persons, institutional racism occurs simply as a result of the normal operations of the major institutions in U.S. society. This type of racism and discrimination can take place without any individual making an effort to hurt those of another race.[1]

Vincent Parrillo, a leading scholar in race and ethnic relations, describes institutional discrimination as behavior that "thoroughly infiltrates a society's customs and institutions (economic, educational, legal and political)." It is so ingrained in the normal daily operations of society that it appears natural rather than malicious. In fact, no individual ill will or racial prejudice is necessary for institutional discrimination to occur. People simply need to carry out the regular operations of society.[2]

Institutional racial discrimination in employment provides a good example of how blacks and whites find themselves separated in the United States as a result of the standard practices of the nation's major institutions. Most people rely on connections—family and friends—to find jobs.[3] The vast majority of blacks and whites do not have cross-racial friends or family members. They live separate lives and therefore do not usually know of the same job opportunities.

Moreover, most employers tend to hire people known to them. In the predominantly white-run economy U.S. economy, whites fill most of the positions involving hiring. For the reasons outlined above, they are much more likely to hear and think of whites than blacks as potential employees. Whether accompanied by racial prejudice or not, the typical hiring processes in a white dominated economy leave blacks at a disadvantage.

One of the results of this institutional racism in employment is that blacks are still much more likely to find themselves unemployed or in blue-collar jobs than whites. For decades, the black unemployment rate has been twice that of whites.[4] Many who grow up in poor all-black communities never interact on a regular basis with those who have professional jobs. There are still few blacks in high-status white-collar positions. For instance, while blacks constitute 13 percent of the population in the United States, in 1997 they made up only 3 percent of architects, 4 percent of engineers, 4 percent of physicians, and 3 percent of lawyers.[5] This separation among whites and blacks in the labor market is one of the many forms of institutional racism that perpetuates the society-wide separation between most black and white Americans today.

All the friends in this book have overcome the formidable institutional obstacles to cross-racial friendship formation that now exist in the United States. Unlike most white and black Americans, they consistently interacted as peers[6] with a member of the other race. This interaction made their friendships possible. Their friendships reveal that race, itself, does not prevent friendship formation. However, the relative scarcity of cross-racial friendships indicates that obstacles to interracial relationships continue to exist.

As Tables 5.1 and 5.2 indicate, 90 percent of the white interviewees do not recall ever having serious discussions about race with family members as they grew up and 95 percent are the offspring of parents who did not have any black friends themselves. For most whites, race is simply not an issue of great concern. Few find themselves in settings where they are not part of the majority. Even those who actually do have cross-racial friendships usually establish them in primarily white environments. As discussed in chapter 4, more than 90 percent of the friendships in this book developed in predominantly white settings.

In order to understand why so few black-white friendships exist, one must utilize what C. Wright Mill's referred to as the "sociological imagination"[7] and begin to connect individual problems with structural issues. In doing so, the relationship between individual Americans' lack of cross-racial friendships and the structural impediments that prevent white and black Americans from forming friendships across the racial divide becomes clear. Using the sociological imagination also leads to the realization that goodwill and individual attempts to ignore racial issues (in other words, colorblindness) will not bring about a large number of interracial friendships. No matter how open you are to interracial friendships, you cannot become friends with persons you do not meet. Structural problems require structural solutions. This chapter focuses on the benefits of recognizing and dismantling the institutional barriers that impede interaction between blacks and whites and the creation of more cross-racial friendships in the United States. In doing so, it examines segregation in housing and schools and provides examples of how these institutional divides may be successfully bridged.

Although racial differences are described by some as gifts Americans bring to one another,[8] friendship potential must exist for us to use and benefit from the gifts of diversity in the United States. Since Gordon Allport's seminal work *The Nature of Prejudice*[9] in 1954, social science research has indicated that close ties between members of different racial groups can do much to reduce racial prejudice. In *The Nature of Prejudice,* Allport outlines the intergroup contact hypothesis, which states that intergroup contact may have a positive effect in reducing prejudice if the following four conditions exist: cooperation between the groups, a common goal, equal status of groups during contact, and the support of authority, custom, or law. Thomas Pettigrew, updating Allport's intergroup contact hypothesis, adds a fifth necessary condition to the contact situation—"friendship potential."[10] Pettigrew maintains that prejudice is reduced to a much greater extent when members of ingroups and outgroups form friendships rather than just acquaintanceships or even more fleeting interactions.

The data from this research is consistent with Pettigrew's assertion. As interviewees of both races stated, close friendships enable people to bond with and learn from one another far more than acquaintance relationships. As Lil, a fifty-nine-year-old black woman, stated,

I do tell people at times. When, you know, people make comments and stuff like that, different comments about race. And I say . . . I know [Barbara] loves me and I know I love her. . . . You know, if people have made a comment or something about race. I have used her, my relationship with her, as an example . . . that you can love each other for real and not have a different feeling [because of race]. . . . I wouldn't care if . . . somebody stood on one side and said "if you step over that line and go to that white lady then I'll kill you." That wouldn't make a difference to me. I would not deny her at all. (Lil, black, 59)

The sharing of personal information and experiences that is a natural part of friendship formation enables people to understand members of other races much more deeply than acquaintance relationships. However, as noted throughout the previous chapters, there are multiple institutional barriers to cross-racial friendship formation in the United States today.

Segregation and lack of cross-racial communication in schools and the work-place prevent Americans from learning and utilizing diverse racial perspectives. On the other hand, when diversity exists and is handled effectively, learning in the classroom and decision-making in the corporate world becomes enhanced and better rounded. For example, cross-racial friendships in the workplace can provide built-in sounding boards for persons who must deal with members of the other race in personnel matters. Bob and Evan and Janet and Caroline are good examples of individuals who find themselves working more confidently and effectively with members of the other race because of their close interracial friendships.

In a May 2001 article in the *New Republic,* Jeffrey Rosen described a reali-zation about the importance of diversity in the classroom. He related that when a black student voiced his perspective during a class discussion on racial pro-filing, it "changed the way [he and the class] thought about the constitution-ality of racial profiling." In doing so, it profoundly altered Rosen's ideas on the impact of diversity in the classroom. While once a skeptic about the importance of diversity, Rosen now realizes that "there can be a meaningful correlation between racial diversity and diversity of viewpoints in the classroom."[11] A rapidly growing body of empirical research supports Rosen's testimony on the benefits of diversity in institutions of higher education.[12]

A great many studies indicate the importance of diversity in the work world, as well. Diverse workforces are more creative and better equipped to solve problems and effectively market to a diverse population[13] than more homo-geneous workforces. Realizing this, General Motors (GM) wrote a forceful friend-of-the-court brief in support of the University of Michigan as it de-fended its policy of affirmative-action admission policies. GM, like most cor-porations today, relies on colleges and universities to teach its workforce to respect and work effectively with people of all races and ethnicities. Indeed, people of color will compose close to 70 percent of new U.S. employees by 2008.[14] GM's efforts on behalf of affirmative action programs is part of a pattern of pro-affirmative action steps major corporations in the United States have taken over the past twenty years. For instance, when affirmative action pro-grams were under attack by the Ronald Reagan and George H. W. Bush ad-ministrations, the Equal Opportunity Advisory Council (consisting of more than 270 companies) and the National Association of Manufacturers managed to turn back these administrations' attempts to alleviate affirmative action re-quirements for companies that conduct business with the federal government.[15]

Six of the friendship pairs in this book formed when their members met at work. The diversity of the workforces gave these individuals the opportunity to form close cross-racial friendships. In turn, these friendships enabled each of them to work more capably with other colleagues. These friendships support the argument that black-white friendships in the workplace benefit both the company and the individuals involved.

According to Patricia Gurin, whose expert report was part of the testimony defending affirmative action at the University of Michigan, students who interact with racially and ethnically diverse persons in college are more likely to live and work in heterogeneous settings than those who do not. However, negative interactions between races and ethnicities are also likely to rise when diversity on college campuses, work sites, or any other institutional setting increases.[16] Therefore, it is important that leaders of such organizations take steps to ensure environments that promote respectful dialogue and openings for friendships across racial and ethnic lines.

INSTITUTIONAL OBSTACLES TO FRIENDSHIP FORMATION

The sociological imagination enables us to understand why so few close cross-racial friendships exists, despite the benefits they provide for society. As noted throughout earlier chapters, our friendships are largely based on proximity. We are much more likely to become friends with people we interact with every day than those we see fleetingly. The manner in which our society is structured prevents large numbers of black and white Americans from ever closely interacting with one another.

The greatest impediment to interracial friendship formation in the United States is racial segregation in neighborhoods and schools. While a 2001 report by the Brookings Institute indicates that housing segregation among whites and blacks has declined somewhat over the last thirty years, the authors of that study still remark that the "large number of American metropolitan areas with extremely high levels of segregation remains quite striking."[17] According to this report, the decreases in segregation are primarily the results of blacks moving into formerly all-white areas. This is seen most often in high-growth areas where blacks made up only a small proportion of the population in 1990. The fact that the change occurs primarily from blacks moving into white areas in places with rapid economic growth lends further credence to Steinhorn and Diggs-Brown's assertion[18] that newly integrated neighborhoods are merely in transition from white to black. If these areas are simply changing from predominantly white to predominantly black, this trend will more likely promote racial resentment than increased opportunities for cross-racial friendships.

Housing

Jan, a fifty-year-old white interviewee, describes the fine line between the benefits of diversity and the fear of neighborhood decline in areas becoming racially mixed:

The neighborhood we've been living in for like seventeen years is very racially mixed. And, to me, that's always been a good thing. . . . [I wanted my kids] to be more aware of other cultures than I was when I grew up and I think there's an enriching experience in that. Now, you know, the bad side of this, and it sounds like I'm saying two things at once and maybe I am. The bad side of that is the neighborhood is getting real black now and it, unfortunately, it does affect property values. It does, somehow, affect crime. I don't know exactly why. We've had lots and lots of families move out [there] from the inner city. . . . And I don't know why crime seems to follow around the movements of black people. . . . But we have moved [out of that neighborhood] recently. . . . But the more you're separated, the more you distrust, the more you're afraid of the unknown or the thing that's different about someone. And we have a hard time accepting people that we don't know very well. (Jan, white, 50)

While Jan expresses a desire to live in an integrated neighborhood and clearly understands the benefits of breaking down mistrust by living among diverse groups of people, her experience has also reinforced her belief that "crime seems to follow around the movements of black people." Middle-class herself, Jan points out that "lots and lots" of blacks from the inner city are moving into her neighborhood. However, Jan does not make a connection based on class: between relatively poor people moving into her neighborhood and increasing crime rates and lowering housing values. She focuses solely on the race of her new neighbors. For Jan, it might have been helpful to join with her neighbors to find out why so many poor people bought homes in what was a middle-class residential area and if redlining was involved. Currently, Jan's former neighborhood is a good example of what Steinhorn and Diggs-Brown[19] described as the eventual fate of almost all neighborhoods that experience an influx of African Americans.

Very few successfully integrated areas exist in the United States. The Walt Disney Corporation's planned city, Celebration, is the most widely known recent integration failure.[20] Despite what Disney describes as concerted efforts to ensure racial and ethnic diversity, the 2000 Census revealed that the community is 88 percent white, 7 percent Hispanic, and 1 percent black, whereas the area surrounding Celebration is 29 percent Hispanic and 6 percent black. While Disney hired black persons to work in Celebration's housing office and advertised in newspapers and magazines with wide circulation among minorities, critics of Disney charge that more efforts should have been made. For example, they point out that Disney gave money to the surrounding county for subsidized housing but did not do enough to ensure affordable housing in Celebration itself.

Celebration is relatively unique in that it is a newly founded city (1994). Most locations that respond to issues of residential diversity must deal with changes to established neighborhoods. Residential areas that undergo racial transformations confront many issues, including redlining and white fear of blacks of any economic means moving into their neighborhood. Shaker Heights, Ohio, and Philadelphia's West Mount Airy neighborhood are among the very few communities that continue to find ways to keep their neighborhoods racially integrated and economically stable. These areas that have successfully managed racial diversity reveal that institutional obstacles, once recognized, may be overcome and provide models for other communities to emulate.

Shaker Heights, Ohio

In Shaker Heights, a coalition of public and nonprofit interests encourage persons shopping for homes to buy in areas where their race is underrepresented. Efforts include advertising, coordination with real-estate agencies and landlords, and providing low-interest loans for those who agree to purchase homes "pro-integratively."[21] Blacks first started to move into Shaker Heights, a relatively affluent suburb of Cleveland, in the late 1950s and 1960s. When this migration occurred, neighborhood associations formed to offset the redlining that real-estate agents had begun to practice. These organizations skirted the agents by appealing directly to potential white buyers and renters and suggesting that blacks move into areas where relatively few blacks were moving.

The city of Shaker Heights took over these efforts of local nonprofit organizations in 1967. Since that time, pro-integrative housing has been one of the major efforts of the city. The city's Pro-Integrative Housing Office uses the successful integration of Shaker Heights as an advertisement for those seeking a stable and diverse area in which to live. The office continues the tradition of personally showing white and black prospective buyers and renters housing in areas where their presence will work to maintain a racial balance in the neighborhood. In short, the nonprofit and public interests of Shaker Heights have worked together, effectively, to engineer the integration of the city. In doing so, they have avoided the panic selling and redlining that took place in many cities and towns throughout the United States since the late 1950s.[22]

West Mount Airy, Philadelphia[23]

West Mount Airy, a neighborhood in Philadelphia, also thwarted forces that led to redlined and segregated neighborhoods surrounding it. Since 1980, the area has consistently remained approximately 50 percent white and 50 percent black. Demographic, environmental, and organizational factors play roles in keeping the neighborhood integrated. Demographically, the white population consists of disproportionate numbers of highly educated persons with above-average median salaries. Whites with relatively high incomes and education levels are more likely to be socially tolerant than poorer, less well educated whites[24] and have less reason to feel financially threatened when blacks begin to buy homes in their neighborhoods. Moreover, the black population that began to purchase houses in Mount Airy in the 1950s was predominantly middle-class, capable of maintaining homes, and therefore not a rational threat to the property values in the neighborhood.

Environmentally, the housing stock in Mount Airy is diverse, attractive, and low in density. The neighborhood, while in a city, has a suburban feel to it, with a park and spaces between homes. The beauty of the neighborhood was an incentive for whites to stay and the distance between homes eased their assent to racial diversity in the general area. Research indicates that persons living in neighborhoods with more open spaces are generally more accepting of diversity than those whose dwellings are closer together.[25]

As in Shaker Heights, organizational factors also contribute to the successful integration of West Mount Airy. West Mount Airy Neighbors (WMAN) came together in 1959 to deal with the racial integration of the neighborhood. Among other activities, the organization has prevented redlining by real-estate agents, received more funding for its schools through participation in the city's desegregation program, and educated the people of the neighborhood so that they would not succumb to panic selling. Today, WMAN is still an active organization that works to unite the diverse residents of West Mount Airy. The strong religious community has also organized effectively across denominations to urge whites to remain. Other nonprofit organizations, such as Mount Airy Learning Tree, continue to bring neighbors of different races, genders, and socioeconomic backgrounds together, offering classes ranging from the history of Mount Airy to computer literacy.

Finally, both West Mount Airy and Shaker Heights have become, in some ways, self-fulfilling prophecies. The local and national publicity the neighborhood and city have received for their successful integration has become a source of pride for their residents and brought an influx of people seeking to live there who appreciate and are comfortable with racial diversity. Blacks come largely for practical reasons, such as the relatively good public schools and nice neighborhoods. Many socially conscious whites come for the experience of living in a successfully integrated neighborhood. The result of the interaction of all these factors is the diminishment of the institutional barrier to black-white friendships that is firmly established in most housing markets in the United States.

Schools

The successful integration of any area relies heavily upon the quality of its school system. School and residential integration directly affect one another. School systems that manage diversity well and produce high-achieving students are a selling point for prospective buyers and a calming influence on whites who may be wary of an influx of blacks into their neighborhoods. If they note that the school system is handling the integration of the races well, they may also appreciate their new neighbors, realizing that the level of integration in an area directly affects the ability of the public schools to provide a racially diverse learning environment.

According to a July 2001 study by the Civil Rights Project at Harvard University, public elementary and high schools in the United States have grown increasingly segregated. More than two-thirds of black and more than one-third of Hispanic students go to schools that are predominantly minority. White students are even more likely to attend racially homogeneous schools. The average white public school student goes to a school where more than four out of five students are white.[26]

While there are fewer racial minorities in private than in public schools, students interact interracially more in private schools than they do in public schools. The two primary reasons appear to be that students attending private schools tend to come from a cross section of neighborhoods, and the religious message of the religiously run private schools influences the students' willingness to interact across racial lines (76.5 percent of primary and secondary private schools are religious.)[27] In a nationwide sample of students, 31 percent of private school students but only 18 percent of public school pupils "strongly agreed that students at their schools made cross-racial friends."[28]

The fact that there are relatively few children of color in private schools compared to public schools may also encourage cross-racial friendships. There are indications that white students do not feel threatened by a small number of racial minority students in their midst and thus do not hesitate to become friends with them. Some research warns of a possible "tipping effect" in which segregation increases as larger numbers of a minority group move into an area.[29] Researchers variously estimate that a "tipping point" occurs when minorities begin to make up either approximately 20 or 30 percent of the total population. Moreover, the racial-minority students in private schools, like many of the black friends in this book, may have the stark choice of having white friends or few friends at all. In any event, most white and black parents depend upon the public school system to educate their children.

Shaker Heights:[30] An Integrated Public School System

Even in relatively diverse cities, it takes constant effort to ensure that the schools are racially integrated. For example, Shaker Heights, Ohio devotes a tremendous amount of resources and social engineering efforts to promote the successful integration of the schools.[31] The school system comprises one high school (grades 9–12), one middle school (grades 7–8), and one upper elementary school (grades 5–6). Formerly, there were nine K–4 schools. Until 1987 four out of the nine were racially segregated.[32] In 1987 the K–4 schools were consolidated into five because enrollments had declined. The district lines were drawn so as to ensure that the racial makeup of each would be relatively comparable to that of the district as a whole.

The overall racial composition of the school system from 1991/1992 through 2000/2001 indicates a city struggling but succeeding in its efforts to keep the schools reasonably evenly mixed. In 1991/1992, 48.1 percent of students in the city school district were black and 47.9 percent were white. By 2000/2001, with more nonblack students of color in the district, 51.2 percent were black and

41.9 percent were white. However, the racial balance of the student population has remained almost unchanged from 1998–2001. In fact, the only change in the most recent data available (2000/2001) reveals the white student population increasing slightly and the black student population decreasing slightly.

This remarkable stability over the past few years in the percentages of whites and blacks may be the result of stricter monitoring of residency requirements for students. The Shaker Heights City School District has an excellent reputation, and many parents from the predominantly black neighboring communities would like to see their sons and daughters benefit from such an education. The strict monitoring of residency requirements since the second half of the 1990s has made it much harder for nonresidents to attend Shaker Heights schools and prevented greater increases in the number of black students.

As Gurin and other social scientists have pointed out,[33] racial interactions in diverse environments must be carefully managed to ensure positive results. Aside from carefully monitoring the numbers of blacks and whites in its school and the validity of the residency claims of its students, the Shaker Heights City School District has also established programs that focus on increasing interaction between the races and the academic success of all students. The Student Group on Race Relations (SGORR) is an organization of high school students who create and organize presentations on the value of cultural and racial diversity for elementary school students. Its brochure describes SGORR as "nationally—in fact, *internationally*—recognized as a model for human relations training." The teams of high school students are purposefully racially diverse. Every year, veteran SGORR students select new student participants for this very popular activity. More than 200 high school students volunteer to be a part of SGORR each year. While modeling positive race relations for elementary school students, the high school students interact closely and often form close cross-racial friendships.

White students of all ages are more likely to pay attention and give effort to their studies than their black classmates, who run the risk of being labeled with such epithets as "oreo" and "sellout" if they excel academically.[34] In order to assist all students in need of assistance and to combat potential disparities between white and black student success, the Shaker Heights City School District has established programs from kindergarten through high school to help students who may be falling behind their classmates. Students are monitored throughout their Shaker Heights student career to ensure that they have the opportunity to succeed scholastically.

While black Shaker Heights high school students have lagged behind their white classmates in grade point average, in 1990, the Minority Achievement Committee Scholars Program was created to address the myth that academic success is for whites only. Minority Achievement Committee scholars are high-achieving black seniors who act as mentors for black underclassmen and motivate them to understand the importance of good grades. In seeing their example, underclassmen are able to see direct evidence that success in school is not a "white thing."[35] Students having difficulty with schoolwork may turn to such resources as after-school tutoring centers, homework centers, the Transition program for freshman in high school who seemed to underperform in middle school, and the Bridges program for students in honors and college preparatory classes. These efforts appear to be working. The high school is recognized as one of the nation's finest.[36]

Not only do these labors seem to be yielding results in scholastic achievement, they also seem to be reaping material rewards for residents of Shaker Heights. Between 1990 and 2000, the average price of a home in Shaker Heights increased an average of 45.6 percent.[37] This success is largely due to the efforts of all sectors of the Shaker Heights community to facilitate their residential and scholastic racial integration. Whites and persons of color are willing to spend increasing amounts of money to live in this area they see as providing a positive environment and a good educational system.

While there is still a gap between black and white achievement, Shaker Heights has proven that money and commitment can yield positive, though not perfect, results in racial integration. However, Shaker Heights has many advantages over most U.S. cities. Both its white and black residential populations are relatively prosperous and the Shaker Heights school system has the money it needs for extensive intervention programs. Shaker Heights also has a more highly educated population than most cities in the United States. The combination of higher education levels, incomes, and property values has led to a relatively wealthy school system with parents who have a keen interest and ability to become involved in their children's academic success. Finally, the racial tension that stems from financial competition between racial groups and hinders cross-racial friendship formation has little fuel in a city where most black and white residents are at least middle-class.

Diversity Within Colleges and Universities

Today, higher education in the United States is in a unique position to provide positive racially diverse environments with wide opportunities for cross-racial friendship formation. Approximately two-thirds of all American high school seniors go directly to college. As an undergraduate degree becomes increasingly vital for success in the twenty-first-century economy, these numbers are expected to continue to increase. A 1999 report for *National College Week,* for example, maintains that full-time undergraduate enrollment will increase by almost 11 percent by 2009.[38] Diversity within colleges and universities is especially crucial considering that it is in college that most students first experience membership in a racially and ethnically heterogeneous institution. Most students' primary and secondary schools are relatively racially homogeneous. Moreover, most of those who do attend racially mixed schools do not actually interact with members of another race in school. Many black teenagers are in the immersion-emersion stage of racial identity discussed in chapter 2, which Cross refers to as the Blacker-than-thou syndrome during which friendships with whites is a sign of a lack of blackness.[39] The peer pressure and flak that many young people face when they do try to establish relationships across racial lines makes crossing the racial divide particularly difficult in high school.[40]

College, however, provides an exceptional opportunity to foster close cross-racial friendships. While many young adults may enter college in stages of racial identity[41] that do not promote extensive interracial interaction, they step into an environment in which interracial interaction is both more possible and more acceptable than at any other point in their lives. Since the benefits of diversity in higher education for both whites and minority students emerged in the mid- to late 1990s,[42] many colleges and universities across the nation have been working harder to increase the racial and ethnic diversity of their student bodies and faculty.[43] Some have gone so far as to project unrealistic pictures of racial diversity on campus in order to attract more minority students. The University of Wisconsin, the University of Idaho, and Auburn University have all superimposed faces of black students on those of whites in student brochures and Web pages in order to project images of a diverse student population in their effort to encourage more minority students to enroll on their campuses.[44]

The Association of American Colleges and Universities recently stated that "diversity is an integral part of educational excellence."[45] According to a 2000 survey cited in the *Chronicle of Higher Education,* 54 percent of colleges and universities have at least one required diversity course and 8 percent more said they were in the process of implementing such a requirement.[46] A 2000 report by the American Association of University Professors notes that more than 60 percent of the top twenty-eight liberal-arts colleges in the United States mention "learning perspectives from diversity" and 57 percent discuss "tolerance and respect for others" in their mission statements and supporting documents.[47]

These figures indicate a growing realization among leaders of institutions of higher learning that it is their responsibility to teach students the skills necessary to act appropriately and succeed in an increasingly diverse society. For example, university officials increasingly state that simply teaching students accounting is not enough to prepare them to work in an accounting firm whose staff and clients are composed of diverse racial and ethnic groups. Employees must be both comfortable and adept at working with people from different races and cultural backgrounds.

However, while diversity classes may spark some students to actively think about and recognize races and cultures other than their own, they are not a replacement for interracial friendships. Neither does a diverse campus necessarily foster many close cross-racial friendships. In fact, some institutions that

succeed in recruiting more minority students to campus may actually experience the tipping effect, leading to increased polarization between races.[48]

In sum, there are more encouraging than discouraging effects of diversity
on college and university campuses. According to a 1999 report by Debra Humphreys for the Ford Foundation Campus Diversity Initiative, students in institutions of higher learning are not, for the most part, self-segregating themselves by race.[49] While there is some clustering going on among students of
color seeking support from one another, most minority students have a racially
and ethnically diverse set of friends. In fact, some students sense that balkan-
ization is occurring when it is not. For instance, in a 1999 study of student
interaction at the University of California at Los Angeles (UCLA), more than
90 percent of students surveyed reported that their classmates tend to socialize
within racial and ethnic groups. However, just 17 percent of UCLA students
indicated that their own friendships were confined to their respective racial and
ethnic backgrounds.[50] White students, reflecting their experiences in largely
white environments prior to college, have the most segregated friendship patterns of all students on college campuses today.[51]

Like the public and nonprofit groups in Shaker Heights and West Mount
Airy, leaders on campus communities must carefully engineer the racial integration they seek. More than requiring students to take diversity classes, they
must arrange campus life so that students of different races interact in situations with friendship potential. In order to do that, administrators must actively
guide housing arrangements and social and event programming on campus to
ensure such an environment.

In a 1993 study of Berkeley undergraduates,[52] Troy Duster found that white
and black students, while both interested in increasing their interaction, were
attracted to different means of getting to know classmates of a different race.
While black students appreciated structured interaction, the white students
tended to want to have more personal and less formal means of spending time
and forming friendships with black classmates. A 1995 Diversity Study by the
University of Maryland revealed similar differences in opinions between its
white and black students.[53] These findings indicate that institutions of higher
learning must find a way to balance the differing tastes of racial groups on
campus and take care not to offend either group with efforts to promote greater
interracial interaction.

Beverly Daniel Tatum, Professor and Dean of Mount Holyoke College and
an expert in the field of diversity in higher education, has created what she
calls the "ABCs" of healthy diverse campuses: "affirming identity, building
community, and cultivating leadership."[54] In order to affirm their sense of identity, every student must see himself or herself represented at his or her college
or university. Students should see themselves reflected in the faculty, fellow
students, and curriculum. Tatum suggests that cultural centers are an important
way that minority groups can gain a sense of belonging to and commitment
for their college or university. Students who know that there is a space

particularly for them on campus are more likely to want to participate in all aspects of their schools, including getting to know fellow students of different racial and ethnic backgrounds.

Joan, a twenty-eight-year-old black interviewee raised in a largely segregated midwestern city, spoke of how attending a university that emphasizes diversity both numerically and programmatically profoundly influenced her perspective on her own racial background and diversity in general:

Coming out here and seeing all these different people and seeing all these different cultures and all these people loving their cultures, I started to love mine even more. And also, out here. . . . differences were praised instead of put down. So, I kind of got into that and started loving that. (Joan, black, 28)

Joan's statement supports Tatum's point that students who feel their own identity affirmed will become more comfortable around and eager to know people of other races and ethnicities.

As Tatum explains, affirming identity is a stepping-stone to building a sense of community among members of diverse groups on campus. While minority students must see places for themselves on campus, she notes that it is also critical that white students not feel ignored in the process. It is important to make the cultures and various backgrounds of white students apparent to all students. The message must be that everyone's heritage is an integral part of the campus community. This can be done, for instance, through the researching and public sharing of students' family histories. In the classroom, community building across races can take place when students of different racial groups are assigned to the same discussion or research groups. Social psychologists like Elliot Aronson have shown that this type of cooperative learning experience can decrease racial stereotypes and increase positive feelings between members of different racial groups.[55] According to Tatum, it is vital that students are encouraged to discuss racial issues openly and often in classrooms. In order to build a sense of community across racial lines, the barriers between various student groups must be broken down through effective communication.

Finally, Tatum adds, institutions of higher learning must cultivate leaders who will be able to act effectively in a diverse society. Tatum offers the Intergroup Relations, Conflict, and Community Program at the University of Michigan as an effective example of how to use both curricular and extracurricular activities to teach students to capably handle diverse situations. The academic courses in this program include intergroup dialogues and student leadership training. Students who wish to lead intergroup dialogues must first pass a three-credit one-semester training course. The following semester they lead groups of twelve to sixteen students, equitably divided between members of two identity groups, through structured discussions.[56] Throughout this program, students learn from their active interactions with one another as well as the purely content oriented aspects of their course work.

Various colleges and universities have enacted similar programs across the country. Arizona State University and the University of Maryland are two universities that are making such efforts to increase positive interaction between students of diverse races. Arizona State University, while composed mainly of white students (71.5 percent white, 10.9 percent Hispanic, 4.9 percent Asian, 3.1 percent African American),[57] has a very active Intergroup Relations Center. The center grew out of student mobilization in response to intergroup hate incidents on campus in 1996. Now sponsored by the office of the Senior Vice-President and the Provost, the center offers both curricular (small group seminar course on issues of diversity) and extracurricular programs (such as an Intergroup Dialogues Program, intergroup theater and musical programs, leadership training in issues of diversity) to encourage students to engage in intergroup dialogue.[58]

The University of Maryland at College Park provides a similar program and curriculum. The university has taken many steps to create a racially and ethnically diverse campus environment. Racial and ethnic minorities now make up one-third of the student undergraduate population (15.1 percent Asian, 13.9 percent African American, and 4.4 percent Hispanic). Concerned about how well the racial and ethnic groups interact, the university carried out a university-wide survey of students' attitudes on diversity on campus in 1999. Immediately thereafter, the university developed the Student Intercultural Learning Center as a response to the needs expressed by the students surveyed. The Student Intercultural Learning Center has created means for students from different races and cultures to interact with one another through a variety of venues (such as intergroup dialogues, peer mediation programs, academic courses exploring diversity through literature and video art) and has established programs to train students to lead their classmates in intercultural dialogues.

Like Arizona State University's efforts, those of the University of Maryland are multifaceted and follow Tatum's ABCs of "affirming identity, building community, and cultivating leadership."[59] Both these universities actively strive to affirm students from all racial and ethnic backgrounds and create a sense of community among undergraduates through dialogue at multiple levels. Moreover, each institution develops student leaders capable of interacting effectively in multicultural surroundings. While these programs were not designed specifically with interracial friendship formations in mind, they have both created environments where the normal institutional barriers to such friendships are diminished.

The positive ramifications of successfully facilitating intercultural/racial interactions on college campuses such as those described above are numerous. Such efforts lead to increased opportunities for interracial friendships and enable young Americans to feel comfortable discussing race and dealing with diversity. As Gurin[60] has noted, these campuses develop graduates more likely to live and work effectively among members of different races and ethnicities. In turn, this increased interaction creates greater structural opportunities for cross-racial friendships. In short, what successful intercultural programming on college campuses can do is to create generations of young adults increasingly capable of crossing the racial divide and effectively using the gifts of the multi-racial population of the United States.

These examples underscore the thesis of this chapter. Individual exertions, alone, will not lead to significantly larger numbers of black-white friendships. While personal efforts are important, they will not be effective unless coupled with institutional change. Today, structural forces separate most black and white Americans from one another. Most never have the opportunity to personally interact with a member of the other race.

The institutional barriers to cross-racial friendships are entrenched in the United States. However, the examples of successful integration in neighborhoods, public primary and secondary schools, and higher education outlined above indicate that these obstacles can be overcome. The social engineering efforts in Shaker Heights, West Mount Airy, and various institutions of higher learning reveal that the institutional divide can be bridged. Moreover, they provide irrefutable evidence that race itself is no barrier to friendship. An essential ingredient to cross-racial friendship formation is opportunity.

NOTES

1. Nijole Benokraitis and Joe Feagin, "Institutional Racism: A Critical Assessment of Literature and Suggestions for Extending the Perspective." pp. 121–43 in *Black /Brown/White Relations*, ed. Charles V. Willie (New Brunswick, NJ: Transaction Books, 1977); Jenny Williams, "Redefining Institutional Racism," *Ethnic and Racial Studies* 8 (1985): 323–48; Leonard Beeghley, *The Structure of Social Stratification in the United States* (Needham: Allyn & Bacon, 2000).

2. Vincent N. Parrillo, *Contemporary Social Problems*, 5th ed., (Boston: Allyn & Bacon, 2002), p. 215.

3. Margaret Grieco, *Keeping It in the Family: Social Networks and Employment Chance* (New York: Travistock, 1987); Lydia Morris, "The Social Segregation of the Long-Term Unemployed in Hartlepool," *Sociological Review* 40 (1992): 344–69.

4. "Improving the Collection and Use of Racial and Ethnic Data in HHS" (Washington, D.C.: Department of Health and Human Services, 1999). Accessed at http://aspe.hhs.gov/datacncl/racerpt/chap7.htm.

5. U.S. Bureau of the Census, "Black Population in the United States, March 1997," *Current Population Reports*, pp. 20–508 (Washington, DC: U.S. Government Printing Office).

6. Aside from the two friendship pairs that began as student–tutor relationships.

7. C. Wright Mills, *The Sociological Imagination* (Oxford, England: Oxford University Press, 1959).

8. See, for instance, Cardinal Francis E. George's pastoral letter on racism, "Dwell in My Love," accessed at http://www.archdiocese-chgo.org/cardinal/dwellinmylove/dwellinmylove.shtm; Mary Robinson, "Tolerance and Diversity: A Vision for the 21st Century" (Geneva, Switz.: United Nations High Commission for Human Rights, 2001), accessed at http://www.parish-without-borders.net/cditt/jp/tolerance-unhchr.htm; and

"A Vision for Bridgewater State College: Diversity" (Bridgewater, MA: Bridgewater State College, 2001), accessed at http://www.bridgew.edu/President/VisionAdrianTinsley.

9. Gordon Allport, *The Nature of Prejudice* (New York: Doubleday, 1954).

10. Thomas F. Pettigrew, "Generalized Intergroup Contact Effects on Prejudice," *Annual Review of Psychology* 49 (1997): 65–85; Pettigrew, "Intergroup Contact Theory." *Personality and Social Psychology Bulletin* 23, 2 (1998): 173–85.

11. Rosen, Jeffrey, "Without Merit." *New Republic*, May 14, 2001, pp. 20.

12. For instance, see the expert report of Patricia Gurin in *Gratz et al. v. Bollinger et al.*, No. 97–75321(E.D. Mich.) and *Grutter et al. v. Bollinger et al.*, No. 97–75928 (E.D. Mich.), and William Bowen and Derek Bok, *The Shape of the River: Long Term Consequences of Considering Race in College and University Admissions* (Princeton, NJ: Princeton University Press, 1998).

13. Barbara Reskin, *The Realities of Affirmative Action in Employment* (Washington, DC: American Sociological Association, 1998); C. Nemeth, "Differential Contributions of Majority and Minority Influence," *Psychological Review* 93 (1986): 23–32.

14. According to the Bureau of Labor Statistics as cited in Jordan Pine, "Reach of School Segregation May Extend into the Future Workplace," *DiversityInc.com*, July 12, 2001.

15. Barbara R. Bergmann, *In Defense of Affirmative Action* (New York: Basic Books, 1996).

16. See Korgen et al. (2001); J. M. Blalock, *Toward a Theory of Minority-Group Relations* (New York: Wiley, 1967); T. H. Cox, *Cultural Diversity in Organizations: Theory, Research and Practice* (San Francisco: Berrett-Koehler, 1993).

17. Edward Glaeser and Jacob Vigdor, "Racial Segregation in the 2000 Census: Promising News" (Brookings Institute Center on Urban and Metropolitan Policy, April 2001). Accessed at http://www.brook.edu/dybdocroot/es/urban/census/glaeserexsum.htm.

18. Leonard Steinhorn and Barbara Diggs-Brown, *By the Color of Our Skin: The Illusion of Integration and the Reality of Race* (New York: Putnam, 2000).

19. Ibid.

20. Jayson Blair, "Failed Disney Vision: Integrated City," *New York Times*, Sept. 23, 2001, p. A31.

21. The low-interest mortgage fund for integrative housing was established in 1985 with a combination of foundation grants and funds from local donors.

22. For an excellent description of redlining, see Hillel Levine and Lawrence Harmon, *The Death of an American Jewish Community: A Tragedy of Good Intentions* (New York: Free Press, 1993).

23. Unless otherwise noted, the information on Mount Airy comes from Barbara Ferman, Theresa Singleton, and Don DeMarco, "West Mount Airy, Philadelphia," *Cityscape* 4, 2 (1998): 29–59.

24. Gabe Wang and Kathleen Korgen, "Social Distance and College Students at a Northern New Jersey University," pp. 95–107 in *The Quality of Contact: African Americans and Whites on College Campuses*, ed. Robert Moore (New York: University Press of America, 2002); Victoria L. Guthrie, Patricia King, and Carolyn Palmer, "Higher Education and Reducing Prejudice: Research on Cognitive Capabilities Underlying Tolerance," *Diversity Digest*, Spring/Summer 2000. Accessed at http://www.diversityweb.org/Digest/Sp.Sm00/contents.html; Jerry Vincent Nix, "Assessing the Existence of Social Distance and Factors That Affect Its Magnitude at a Southern

University," sspp.net vol. 1, 1997–1999. Accessed at http://www.sspp.net/archive/papers/nix.htm.

25. Leonard Heumann, "The Definition and Analysis of Stable Racial Integration: The Case of West Mount Airy, Philadelphia" (Ph.D. diss., University of Pennsylvania, Philadelphia, 1973); Juliet Saltman, *A Fragile Movement: The Struggle for Neighborhood Stabilization* (Westport, CT: Greenwood Press, 1990).

26. Gary Orfield, "Schools More Separate: Consequences of a Decade of Resegregation" (Cambridge, MA: Harvard University, 2001). Accessed at http://www.researchmatters.harvard.edu/story.php?article_id=268&section=society.

27. Stephen P. Broughman and Lenore A. Colaciello, "Private School Universe Survey: 1999–2000," *Education Statistics Quarterly* 3, 4 (Fall 2001). Accessed at http://nces.ed.gov/pubs2002/quarterly/fall/q3–4.asp; Jay P. Greene and Nicole Mellow, "Integration Where It Counts: A Study of Racial Integration in Public and Private School Lunchrooms," paper presented at the meeting of the American Political Science Association, Boston, Sept. 1998.

28. Jay P. Greene, "Why School Choice Can Promote Integration," *Education Week*, April 12, 2000, p. 52.

29. Morton Grodzins, "Metropolitan Segregation," *Scientific American* 197, 24 (Oct. 1957): 33–41; Thomas Schelling, *Micromotives and Macrobehavior* (New York: Norton, 1978); Nathan Glazer, "Black and White After Thirty Years," *Public Interest* 121 (Fall 1995): 61–71.

30. Because Mount Airy is a neighborhood within the city of Philadelphia, it does not have control over its own school system. While Mount Airy schools are ranked higher than most in the city of Philadelphia, a relatively large number of Philadelphia students attend private schools (29 percent of Philadelphia students attended private school in 1990 compared with approximately 20 percent of students in Boston, New York, Chicago, Cleveland, and Cincinnati). Most of the white Mount Airy residents send their children to private schools. Therefore, they are not as invested in the successful integration of the neighborhood schools as they are in the neighborhood itself. For these reasons, Shaker Heights is a better example of a successful attempt at integrating a public school system.

31. The following information comes from a personal conversation with a member of the Shaker Heights School Board and from Lisa Payne Jones, "Report of the Registrar: 1991–92 to 2000–01," Shaker Heights, OH: Shaker Heights City School District, Nov. 2000.

32. The fact that four of the nine neighborhood elementary schools were racially segregated reveals that even Shaker Heights is not perfectly integrated throughout its neighborhoods.

33. The expert testimony of Patricia Gurin *Gratz et al. v. Bollinger et al.*, No. 97–75321(E.D. Mich.) and *Grutter et al. v. Bollinger et al.*, No. 97–75928 (E.D. Mich.). Found at www.umich.edu/~urel/admissions/legal/expert/gurintoc. Gordon Allport, *The Nature of Prejudice* (Garden City, NY: Doubleday, 1954).

34. Pam Belluck, "Reason Is Sought for Lag by Blacks in School Effort," *New York Times*, July 4, 1999, p. A1; Anthony Walton, "Technology Versus African-Americans," *Atlantic Monthly*, Jan. 1999. Accessed at http://www.theatlantic.com/issues/99jan/aftech.htm; Denise F. Noldon and William E. Sedlacek, "A Comparison of Attitudes and Behaviors of Incoming Honors Freshmen by Race and Gender," Research Report

#4–94, University of Maryland Counseling Center, 1994; accessed at http://www .inform.umd.edu/EdRes/Topic/Diversity/General/Reading/Sedlacek/biggi.html.

35. Lynette Clemetson, "Trying to Close the Achievement Gap," *Newsweek*, June 7, 1999, p. 36.

36. Ibid.

37. Citizens' Finance Review Committee. "Report of the Citizens' Finance Review Committee." *Shaker School Review*, Winter 2000, p. 8.

38. "Getting There: A Report for *National College Week*." *National College Week*, Nov. 1999. Accessed at http://www.ed.gov/pubs/CollegeWeek/highlights.html.

39. William E. Cross Jr., *Shades of Black: Diversity in African-American Identity* (Philadelphia: Temple University Press, 1999), p. 205.

40. See chapter 2 for an extensive discussion of how peer pressure in high school can hinder the development of cross-racial friendships.

41. See chapter 2 for a discussion of black racial identity.

42. J. R. Alger, "The Educational Values of Diversity," *Academe* 1 (Jan.–Feb. 1997): 20–23; Bowen and Bok, *The Shape of the River;* and the expert report of Patricia Gurin in *Gratz et al. v. Bollinger et al.*, No. 97–75321(E.D. Mich.) and *Grutter et al. v. Bollinger et al.*, No. 97–75928 (E.D. Mich.)

43. See, for example, the March 1999 report of the University of Rochester's Residential College Commission Subcommittee on Diversity (http://www.lib.Rochester.edu /diversity/divrep.htm) and Bridgewater State College's mission statement on diversity (http://www.bridgew.edu/President/Vision/Diversity.cfm).

44. "Noteworthy News: University of Idaho, Auburn U. Also Report Incidents of Doctored Photos." *Black Issues in Higher Education* (Oct. 26, 2000). Accessed at http: //iibpchadwyck.com/toc/BlackIssuesinHigherEducation/26October2000.htm; Jennifer Jacobson, "In Brochures, What You See Isn't Necessarily What You Get," *Chronicle of Higher Education*, March 16, 2001, p. A41.

45. Association of American Universities and Colleges, "American Commitments: Diversity, Democracy and Liberal Learning," The Association, 1998. Accessed at http: //www.aacu-edu.org/Initiatives/amercommit.html.

46. Elizabeth Greens, "Most Colleges Require Diversity Education," *Chronicle of Higher Education*, Nov. 3, 2000, p. A16.

47. Jonathan Alger et al., "Does Diversity Make a Difference?" American Association of University Professors, May 2000.

48. For a discussion of "tipping" in society, see Grodzins, "Metropolitan Segregation"; Schelling, *Micromotives;* and Glazer, "Black and White." See Kathleen Korgen James Mahon and Gabe Wang, "Diversity on College Campuses Today," *College Student Journal* (forthcoming), for a focus on tipping on college campuses.

49. Debra Humphreys, "Campus Diversity and Student Self-Segregation: Separating Myths from Facts." Diversity Web: An Interactive Resource Hub for Higher Education, Association of American Colleges and Universities and the University of Maryland 1999. Accessed at http://www.diversityweb.org/Leadersguide/SED/studeseg.html.

50. Anthony Lising Antonio, "Racial Diversity and Friendship Groups in College: What the Research Tells Us," *Diversity Digest*, Summer 1999, pp. 6–7, cited in Humphreys, "Campus Diversity."

51. John Matlock, "Student Expectations and Experiences: The Michigan Study," *Diversity Digest*, Summer 1997, p. 11, cited in Humphreys, "Campus Diversity."

52. Troy Duster, "The Diversity of the University of California at Berkeley: An Emerging Reformulation of Competence in an Increasingly Multicultural World," pp. 231–256 in *Beyond a Dream Deferred: Multicultural Education and the Politics of Excellence*, ed. B. W. Thompson and S. Tyagi (Minneapolis: University of Minnesota Press, 1993).

53. Bill Sedlacek, "Diversity Study 1995: Preliminary Summary of Results," *Institutional Profiles: Diversity Research and Evaluation* (College Park: University of Maryland, 1995). Accessed at http://www.diversityweb.org/Profiles/divdbase/umd/DREI/1995_Survey_results.html.

54. Beverly Daniel Tatum, "The ABC Approach to Creating Climates of Engagement on Diverse Campuses," *Liberal Education* 86, 4 (2000): 22–30.

55. E. Aronson, N. Blaney, C. Stephin, J. Sikes, and M. Snapp, *The Jigsaw Classroom* (Beverly Hills, CA: Sage Publications, 1978).

56. Monita C. Thompson, Teresa Graham Brett, and Charles Behling, "Educating for Social Justice: The Program on Intergroup Relations, Conflict, and Community at the University of Michigan," pp. 99–114 in *Intergroup Dialogue*, ed. David Schoem and Sylvia Hurtado. Ann Arbor: University of Michigan Press, 2001.

57. Racial demographics of undergraduates at the main Arizona State campus are from ASU Mainfacts: http://www.asu.edu/Data_Admin/MainFacts/Enrollment.pdf.

58. Unless otherwise noted, the information on Arizona State University's IRC programs comes from the IRC Web site: http://www.asu.edu/provost/intergroup/progmain.html.

59. Tatum, "The ABC Approach."

60. See her expert testimony in *Gratz et al. v. Bollinger et al.*, No. 97–75321(E.D. Mich.) and *Grutter et al. v. Bollinger et al.*, No. 97–75928 (E.D. Mich.). Found at http://www.umich.edu/~urel/admissions/legal/expert/gurintoc.

Conclusion

> I thought that Hispanics and whites and blacks shouldn't be together. I think I thought it was just that way. . . . [But] I've learned my lesson. . . . Cause I know now that everyone can be together. . . . You have to know the person before you say anything. I think that's the thing I learned about it. . . . They don't think they can [be together] and they're just mean to [each other] because they don't know [each other].
>
> Joelle, black, 10

Joelle, a ten-year-old black interviewee,[1] said that she might write a letter to the President of the United States, asking how "we can get . . . more kids to be together from different races." At the age of ten, she has already experienced racial feuds and reconciliations with her classmates in the public school she attends. She believes that the problems between people of different races arise, in large part, "because they don't know each other." Joelle says she has "learned her lesson" and is now eager to share that lesson with others. She thinks that she may join some of her friends of different races to spread their belief that friendships can be formed across the racial divide.

Joelle knows that she cannot, individually, bring all Americans across the racial divide. The reality is that it will take more than personal goodwill to create the opportunities for substantially more cross-racial friendships in our society. Through segregation in our neighborhoods and schools, the structure of our society works to prevent strong cross-racial friendships. Consequently, most blacks and whites never have occasion to interact closely with members of the other race. This study suggests that it will take a concerted effort on the structural and the individual level to greatly increase opportunities for black-white friendship formations in the United States.

Although increasing numbers of Americans maintain that the best solution to racial issues is to become "colorblind" and ignore the impact of race, this research indicates that race, while a social construction, is still a powerful force at all levels of U.S. society—and not a force to be ignored. Colorblind attitudes may help some individuals develop and maintain friendships across the racial divide, yet they do nothing to diminish the divide itself. In order to reduce the racial divide, we must first be able to see it clearly. Once we recognize the institutional, individual, and cultural barriers that currently separate white and black Americans, we can begin to decrease the distance between us.

As discussed in chapter 2, whites often seem to be more accepting of cross-racial friendships than do blacks. Blacks who are in the immersion-emersion stage of racial identity, most often teenagers and young adults, have particularly negative attitudes toward close interracial interaction. On the other hand, many whites look upon platonic friendships between blacks and whites as signs of a healthy society (white views on interracial romantic relationships are much more negative). At the same time, white people are primarily responsible for the institutional reasons that close black-white friendships are so rare. Whether through the legal methods of the past or the de facto means of the present, whites have distanced themselves from blacks throughout the history of the United States. Their current openness to black-white friendships erases neither this history nor the social structures that accompanied it.

The friends in this book who crossed the racial divide provide evidence that race itself is not an obstacle to friendship formation. Even Bob and Evan, who originally perceived each other through negative racial stereotypes, realized, once they were compelled to work closely with each other, that race did not have the power to separate them. After interacting long enough to dispel the stereotypes, the two men realized that they, like the vast majority of the cross-racial friends in this book, had much in common. The formation of the cross-racial friendships in the book followed the typical pattern of most close friendships, with "like attracting like."

While Bob and Evan and ten other interviewees discussed, to various degrees, racial issues with one another, race can be the unspoken "elephant in the living room," even for close friends. Most of the friends rarely spoke seriously about the subject with one another, employing various means to avoid it. Half the friends simply skirted the topic completely. As Kyle, a twenty-three-year-old white college student, put it, "It's not even like something that comes up in . . . conversation" between him and Pat. Others used humor to deal with the taboo subject. Nine pairs of interviewees, mostly male college students, described race as fodder for conversation only when they were making fun of each other. As one interviewee described it, race was not a topic of discussion between them at all except for when they were "like, ripping on each other."

Even those friends who did not actively discuss issues of race have been positively influenced by their close cross-racial friendships. While only eleven white interviewees actively fight racism,[2] all view blacks, as a group, in a more positive light since having a close black friend. All the white interviewees now view blacks as potential friends.

The black interviewees also maintained that their cross-racial friendships have improved their estimation of the other race. For instance, Pam positively contrasted her outlook on racial issues with those of family members who still interact almost exclusively in the black community. While most black inter-viewees, like Pam, have a generally more positive opinion of whites since be-coming close friends with a white person, a sizable minority described dramatic transformations in their beliefs about whites as a result of their cross-racial friendships. One out of four black interviewees said that their close friendship with a white person enabled them to see, for the first time, that there were some good white people.

These results indicate the positive effects cross-racial friendships have and can have on our society. Cross-racial friendships are not a panacea for racism. Instead, what they do is give us the tools we need to alleviate it. As discussed in chapters 5 and 6, those who form friendships across the racial divide are more capable of understanding the perspective of members of the other race than those who do not have a cross-racial friend. This understanding improves their ability to interact with people from diverse backgrounds both personally and professionally. They become more accepting of integration in their neigh-borhoods and more capable of working with and for members of another race at their places of employment. The friendships in this book reveal

that the racial divide can be crossed on the individual level

that the racial divide is a social construction

that the depth of the structural divide still exists between white and black Americans

In order to alleviate the divide on the institutional level, we must desegregate housing and education in the United States. Just as Americans increasingly recognize that the very concept of race is socially constructed, we must now acknowledge the institutional barriers to cross-racial friendships as social cre-ations we can overcome.

Patricia Williams writes "the solution to racism lies in our ability to see its ubiquity but not to concede its inevitability."[3] Cross-racial friendships provide a unique perspective that makes racism both more visible and more vulnerable than ever before. We can make use of this knowledge, however, only if we utilize both our hearts and our minds. If we are to understand how members of other races view the world, we must interact with them with our hearts. We must become friends. A significantly larger number of such friendships will develop only if we also use our minds to recognize the structural impediments to such friendships and work to bridge the institutional racial divide. As Joelle explains, we must have the opportunity to know one another before we can become friends.

NOTES

1. My intent was to interview adults but, given the opportunity, I thought it would be useful to hear the perspective of one pair of friends who were children.

2. Typical antiracist activities of the interviewees were speaking out at antiracism rallies on college campuses, purposefully sitting with blacks at a segregated social gathering, challenging other whites who make racial remarks, and participating in antiracist marches.

3. Patricia J. Williams, *Seeing a Color-Blind Future: The Paradox of Race* (London: Virago Press, 1997), p. 68.

Appendix A

Demographics of Interviewees

	Name	Race	Age	Class[1]	Length of Friendship
1	Steven	black	19	middle	4 years
	Jeff	white	19	lower-middle	4 years
2	Tracy	black	50	middle	22 years
	Carol	white	58	middle	22 years
3	Rod	black	45	middle	31 years
	Vinnie	white	45	middle	31 years
4	Ty	black	24	middle	10 months
	Pete	white	21	middle	10 months
5	Pam	black	53	upper-middle	16 years
	Ellen	white	59	middle	16 years
6	Latrice	black	18	middle	7 months
	Jane	white	20	upper-middle	7 months
7	Ese	black	21	upper-middle	3 years
	Peggy	white	21	upper-middle	3 years
8	Keith	black	21	lower-middle	3 years
	Phil	white	21	middle	3 years
9	Kofi	black	35	middle	13 years
	Dave	white	35	middle	13 years
10	Kathy	black	29	middle	18 years
	Elaine	white	30	middle	18 years
11	Yvette	black	39	lower-middle	16 years
	Cheryl	white	39	lower-middle	16 years
12	Doris	black	49	upper-middle	1 1/2 years
	Hillary	white	50	upper-middle	1 1/2 years
13	Joe	black	18	upper-middle	8 months
	Devin	white	18	middle	8 months
14	James	black	18	middle	9 months
	Vern	white	19	middle	9 months
15	Patrick	black	23	middle	10 years
	Kyle	white	23	middle	10 years
16	Valerie	black	35	middle	8 months
	Kristin	white	37	middle	8 months

(Continued on next page)

17	Janet	black	47	middle	10 years
	Caroline	white	53	upper-middle	10 years
18	Harriet	black	51	middle	About 5 years
	Marie Elena	white	53	middle	About 5 years
19	Lil	black	59	middle	25 - 30 years
	Barbara	white	84	middle	25 - 30 years
20	Liz	black	34	middle	2 years
	Patty	white	37	middle	2 years
21	Kia	black	18	middle	3 years
	Cindy	white	20	middle	3 years
22	Bob	black	43	middle	About 8 years
	Evan	white	41	middle	About 8 years
23	Sandra	black	50	middle	8 years
	Beth	white	50	middle	8 years
24	Charles	black	18	middle	6 months
	Carl	white	18	middle	6 months
25	Martin	black	46	mid-upper-middle	15 years
	Tim	white	48	upper-middle	15 years
26	Chris	black	18	lower	9 months
	Matt	white	18	middle	9 months
27	Vanessa	black	18	middle	8 months
	Mary Anne	white	18	middle	8 months
28	Maria	black	20	middle	3 years
	Tabitha	white	19	middle	3 years
29	Kobe	black	28	low-lower-middle	5 years
	Paula	white	26	middle	5 years
30	Betty	black	46	middle	6 years
	Patricia	white	65	middle	6 years
31	Ebony	black	19	lower	8 years
	Alison	white	34	lower-middle	8 years
32	Joelle	black	10	middle	3 years
	Maura	white	10	lower	3 years
33	Patrice	black	19	lower	7 years
	Mary	white	38	middle	7 years
34	Louise	black	45	middle	6 years
	Elizabeth	white	47	upper-middle	6 years

(Continued on next page)

Appendix A *(continued)*

35	Joan	black	28	middle	23 years
	Jan	white	28	middle	23 years
36	Violet	black	85	middle	about 55 years
	Gert	white	82	middle	about 55 years
37	Ed	black	23	working-middle	2 years
	Arthur	white	23	lower-middle	2 years
38	Nicole	black	21	middle	3 years
	Candace	white	21	middle	3 years
39	Paulette	black	44	middle	1 1/2 years
	Cindy	white	50	middle	1 1/2 years
40	Christina	black	23	lower-middle	8 years
	Paula	white	24	middle	8 years

[1]The economic classes listed here are based on the interviewees' self-definitions of their class.

Appendix B

Notes on Methodology

The data utilized in this book come from semistructured, intensive interviews of forty pairs of black-white close friends, undertaken between 2000 and 2002. The races of the interviewees are their own racial self-definitions. The definition of "close" friends used in this book is friends who would feel comfortable calling each other during the middle of the night, in case of an emergency ("3:00 A.M. friends"). I recruited interviewees through advertisements in university and local newspapers, the snowball method (one interviewee suggesting another), and word of mouth. I found six pairs through the snowball method. Eleven pairs responded to ads placed in newspapers. I also contacted two pairs after reading published articles on their interracial friendships. I offered each interviewee $10, as a token of appreciation.

I found the majority of pairs through friends, acquaintances, and relative strangers, asking whether they knew of any close black-white friendships. Most people I asked were not able to assist me. They did not know of any black-white pairs of friends. Many more were able to suggest romantically involved black-white couples rather than black-white platonic friends. In fact, several members of such couples answered my ads volunteering to be interviewed. However, I confined my interviews to persons involved in platonic close black-white friendships. The vast majority of the friendship pairs consisted of persons of the same gender. Only one pair was composed of a man and a woman.

Participants in the study came from California, Kansas, Massachusetts, Missouri, New Jersey, New York, Rhode Island, Texas, and Wisconsin. I interviewed each friend separately for between one and two hours. Sixty-seven interviews took place in person, at a location convenient for the interviewee (e.g., an office, dorm lounge, coffee shop, restaurant), and thirteen were carried out over the phone. Two of the interviewees were ten-year-old girls; the rest ranged in age from eighteen to eighty-five.

I chose to collect my primary data through interviews for several reasons. Discussions on race are always sensitive. This method of data collection enables the researcher to gain the trust and confidence of the person being interviewed. This, I believe, made it possible to gather more honest and elaborate answers than would have been possible using another methodology, such as a survey. The semistructured format also allowed me to compare answers to questions asked of each interviewee and pursue topics of interest initiated by the various participants. This methodological approach allowed me to adjust my focus when needed and achieve a greater depth of understanding of the influence of race on close friendships between blacks and whites.

Undoubtedly, my own race influenced, to some extent, the responses of the interviewees and my own interpretations of them. I do not believe, however, that one must be either a member of or outside a group in order to study it effectively. As Mary Waters writes in her appendix to *Black Identities: West Indian Immigrant Dreams and American Realities,* "an insider and an outsider will not see exactly the same things or interpret things exactly the same, but that does not make one perspective automatically invalid."[1] On the contrary, I maintain that in order to comprehend a subject, we must be able to view it from as many perspectives as possible. For a description of my own background in relation to this research, please see Appendix C.

The grounded theory approach developed by Glaser and Strauss[2] guided the coding and analysis of the interviews. While I had some tentative hypotheses going into the data collection based upon a review of secondary data sources, historical knowledge, and personal observation, I remained open to whatever findings the data elicited. Glaser and Strauss's approach allowed me to be receptive to ideas that I had not considered before conducting the research.

The following topics were covered in each interview:

- basic demographic information
- background on when and how the friendship began
- each interviewee's self-definition of the strength of the friendship
- views on members of their friend's race before the friendship
- views on members of their friend's race now
- general views on race relations in the United States before the friendship
- general views on race relations in the United States now
- beliefs on how race affects their friendship (if at all)
- reactions of friends, family, acquaintances, strangers, to the friendship
- whether race was discussed in household of origin
- whether issues of race are discussed between the friends
- race of the interviewee's parents' friends
- whether the interviewee is/has been prejudiced/practiced discrimination against members of another race (if so, what race(s) and why)
- how the interviewee feels about his or her own race generally
- whether the interviewee feels connected to members of his or her own race. What is the racial makeup of the interviewee's other friends? How close these friendships are.

- if the interviewee were going to a racially (black/white) divided party where the interviewee did not know anyone, where would the interviewee go? Why?
- whether the interviewee or the friend has any advantages or disadvantages due to race (compared to the other)

NOTES

1. Mary C. Waters, *Black Identities: West Indian Immigrant Dreams and American Realities* (Cambridge, MA: Harvard University Press, 1999), p. 363.

2. Barney G. Glaser and Anselm Strauss, *The Discovery of Grounded Theory* (Chicago: Aldine, 1967).

Appendix C

Notes on the Author

I am a white woman who does not have a close black friend. I have dated a black man, but that involved different issues from those that face close, platonic black-white friends. I have a nephew of mixed (black-white) descent whom I adore. There are colleagues and other people in my life I have met in recent years whom I consider friends, who happen to be black. However, I would not refer to them as *close* friends. Not one of the people I might call up in case of a 3:00 A.M. emergency is black.

In fact, as a tenure-track assistant professor with a two-year-old daughter and another on the way, I find it hard to keep up the close friendships I have developed over the years. I tend to have little time to connect with people, beyond my immediate family, outside of work. I know the time crunch I face is not unique. A scarcity of outside-work socialization is common today. Many people I talked to about this book project confided in me that they are so busy with their families and careers that they have hardly any close friends (but that is material for another book).

The reasons behind my lack of close black friends, despite my interest in and commitment to racial justice, are clearly evident in my background. While my extended family includes many different races and ethnicities, I grew up and went to school with very few black people. I went to public schools in Worcester, Massachusetts, through high school but do not remember a single black student in any of my college-bound classes. I attended elite Catholic institutions for my college and graduate academic work, where the percentages of black students were in the low single digits. My family and I recently moved into a neighborhood that is predominantly made up of mixed-race and black families (and therefore provides opportunities for cross-racial friendships), but the natural opportunities for forming friendships with black people simply did not exist for most of my life. The difficulties I had in finding forty pairs of black-white friends indicate that my largely racially homogeneous upbringing is typical and belies the optimistic headlines concerning interracial friendships discussed in chapter 1 and support the structural arguments made in chapter 6.

Bibliography

Affifi, Walid, and Laura Guerrero. "Some Things Are Better Left Unsaid II: Topic Avoidance in Friendships." *Communication Quarterly* 46, 3 (1998): 231–49.

Alger, J. R. "The Educational Values of Diversity." *Academe* 1 (Jan.–Feb. 1997): 20–23.

Alger, Jonathan, Jorge Chapa, Roxane Harvey Gudeman, Patricia Morin, Geoffrey Maruyama, Jeffrey F. Milem, José F. Moreno, Deborah J. Wilds. "Does Diversity Make a Difference?: Three Research Studies on Diversity in College Classrooms." Office of Minorities in Higher Education, May 2000. Accessed at http://www.acenet.edu/programs/omhe/diversity.cfm.

Allport, Gordon W. *The Nature of Prejudice.* New York: Doubleday, 1954.

Altman, I., and D. A. Taylor. *Social Penetration: The Development of Interpersonal Relationships.* New York: Holt, Rinehart and Winston, 1973.

Angier, Nancy. "Do Races Differ? Not Really, DNA Shows." *New York Times on the Web,* Aug. 22, 2000. Accessed at http://www.nytimes.com/library/national/science/082200sci-genetics-race.html.

Antonio, Anthony Lising. "Racial Diversity and Friendship Groups in College: What the Research Tells Us." *Diversity Digest,* Summer 1999.

Aronson, E., N. Blaney, C. Stephin, J. Sikes, and M. Snapp. *The Jigsaw Classroom.* Beverly Hills, CA: Sage Publications, 1978.

Astor, Charlotte. "Gallup Poll: Progress in Black/White Relations, but Race Is Still an Issue." *USIA Electronic Journal* 2, 3 (Aug. 1997). Accessed at http://usinfo.state.gov/journals/itsv/0897/ijse/gallup.htm.

Bean, Linda. "Analysis: Higher Interest for Blacks but Nissan Denies Bias in Lending." *DiversityInc.com,* July 9, 2001.

Beeghley, Leonard. *The Structure of Social Stratification in the United States.* Boston, MA: Allyn & Bacon, 2000.

Belluck, Pam. "Reason Is Sought for Lag by Blacks in School Effort." *New York Times,* July 4, 1999, p. A11.

Benokraitis, Nijole, and Joe Feagin. "Institutional Racism: A Critical Assessment of Literature and Suggestions for Extending the Perspective." Pp. 121–43 in *Black/Brown/White Relations,* ed. Charles V. Willie. New Brunswick, NJ: Transaction Books, 1977.

Bergmann, Barbara R. *In Defense of Affirmative Action.* New York: Basic Books, 1996.

Bernal, Martin. *Black Athena: The Afroasiatic Roots of Classical Civilization.* Vol. 1, *The Fabrication of Ancient Greece 1785–1985,* Newark NJ: Rutgers University Press, 1987.

Bethel, Alison. "In Living Color: The Newest Bostonians Are Multiracial, Multicultural, and Pleased to Meet You." *Boston Globe,* June 20, 1999, p. A30.

Blair, Jayson. "Failed Disney Vision: Integrated City." *New York Times,* Sept. 23, 2001, p. A31.

Blalock, J. M. *Toward a Theory of Minority-Group Relations.* New York: Wiley, 1967.

Bledsoe, T., S. Welch, L. Sigelman, and M. Combs. "Suburbanization, Residential Integration, and Racial Solidarity Among African Americans." Paper presented at the annual meeting of the Midwest Political Science Association, Chicago, April 1994.

Bobo, Lawrence, and Camille Zubrinsky. "Attitudes on Residential Integration: Perceived Status Differences, Mere In-group Preference, or Racial Prejudice?" *Social Forces* 74, 3 (1996): 883–900.

Bogardus, Emory S. *Social Distance.* Yellow Springs, OH: Antioch, 1959.

Bowen, William, and Derek Bok. *The Shape of the River: Long Term Consequences of Considering Race in College and University Admissions.* Princeton, NJ: Princeton University Press, 1998.

Broughman, Stephen P., and Lenore A. Colaciello. "Private School Universe Survey: 1999–2000." *Education Statistics Quarterly* (Fall 2001). Accessed at http://nces.ed.gov/pubs2002/quarterly/fall/q3–4.asp.

"Brown University Study: Racial Biases Need Acknowledgment." *Masspsy.com* 8, 4 (April 2000). Accessed at http://www.masspsy.com/leading/0004_qa.html.

Brown et al. v. Board of Education of Topeka et al. 347 US 483 (1954).

Citizens' Finance Review Committee. "Report of the Citizens' Finance Review Committee." *Shaker School Review,* Winter 2000, p. 8

Clark, William A. V. "Residential Preferences and Neighborhood Racial Segregation: A Test of the Schelling Segregation Model." *Demography* 28 (1991): 1–19.

Clemetson, Lynette. "Trying to Close the Achievement Gap." *Newsweek,* June 7, 1999, p. 36.

Cooley, Charles Horton. *Human Nature and the Social Order.* New York: Schocken Books, 1902.

Cox, T. H. *Cultural Diversity in Organizations: Theory, Research and Practice.* San Francisco: Berrett-Koehler, 1993.

Cross, William E., Jr. *Shades of Black: Diversity in African-American Identity.* Philadelphia: Temple University Press, 1999.

DeMott, Benjamin. "Put On a Happy Face: Masking the Differences Between Blacks and Whites," *Harper's Magazine,* Sept. 1995, pp. 31–38.

Derlega, V. J., S. Metts, S. Petronio, and S. T. Margulis. *Self-Disclosure.* Newbury Park, CA: Sage Publications, 1993.

"Differences Persist in Views of Race Relations." *Yahoo! News,* July 11, 2001. http://dailynews.yahoo.com/htx/kgtv/20010710/lo/853917_1.html.

"The Diversity Dilemma." *Commonweal,* March 9, 2001, pp. 5, 6.

Doane, Ashley W. Jr. "Dominant Group Ethnic Identity in the United States." *Sociological Quarterly* 38, 3 (Summer 1997): 375–97.

DuBois, W. E. B. *The Souls of Black Folk: Essays and Sketches.* Greenwich, CT: Fawcett, 1961.

Durkheim, Émile. *Suicide.* New York: Free Press, 1997.

Duster, Troy. "The Diversity of the University of California at Berkeley: An Emerging Reformulation of Competence in an Increasingly Multicultural World." Pp. 231–256 in "An Emerging Reformulation of Competence in an Increasingly Multicultural World." *Beyond a Dream Deferred: Multicultural Eduation and the Politics of Excellence*, ed. B. W. Thompson and S. Tyagi. Minneapolis: University of Minnesota Press, 1993.

Ellison, Christopher G., and Daniel A. Powers. "The Contact Hypothesis and Racial Attitudes Among Black Americans." *Social Science Quarterly* 75, 2 (1994): 385–400.

Feagin, Joe R. "The Continuing Significance of Race: Antiblack Discrimination in Public Places." *American Sociological Review* 56 (1991): 101–16.

———. *Racist America*. New York: Routledge, 2000.

Feagin, Joe, and Hernán Vera. *White Racism*. New York: Routledge, 1995.

Ferman, Barbara, Theresa Singleton, and Don DeMarco. "West Mount Airy, Philadelphia." *Cityscape* 4, 2 (1998): 29–59.

Fetto, John. "Interracial Friendships Slip?" *American* Demographics (Jan. 2000). Accessed at http://www.marketingtools.com/publications/as/00_as/001_as/as000106e.htm.

Frankenberg, Ruth. *White Women, Race Matters: The Social Construction of Whiteness*. Minneapolis: University of Minnesota Press, 1993.

Gallup Organization. "Special Reports: Black-White Relations in the United States, 2001 Update." July 10, 2001. Accessed at http://www.gallup.com/poll/specialreports/pollsummaries/sr010711.asp

"Getting There: A Report for *National College Week*." *National College Week*, Nov. 1999. Accessed at http://www.ed.gov/pubs/CollegeWeek/highlights.html.

Glaeser, Edward, and Jacob Vigdor. "Racial Segregation in the 2000 Census: Promising News." *Brookings Institute Center on Urban and Metropolitan Policy*, Survey Series, April 2001. Accessed at www.brook.edu/es/urban/census/glaeser.pdf.

Glaser, Barney G., and Anselm Strauss. *The Discovery of Grounded Theory*. Chicago: Aldine, 1967.

———. *Status Passages*. Chicago: Aldine Atherton, 1971.

Glazer, Nathan. "Black and White After Thirty Years." *Public Interest* 121 (Fall 1995): 61–71.

"Globe Poll: Views on Race in America." *Boston Globe Online*, May 11, 2000. Accessed at www.boston.com/globe/nation/packages/rethinking_integration/views_on_race_poll.htm.

Goffman, Erving. *Interaction Ritual*. New York: Doubleday, 1967.

———. *The Presentation of Self in Everyday Life*. Garden City, NY: Doubleday, 1959.

Gonzales, M. H., J. M. Davis, G. L. Loney, C. K. Kukens, and C. M. Junghans. "Interactional Approach to Interpersonal Attraction." *Journal of Personality and Social Psychology* 44 (1983): 1192–97.

Gottheif, Michelle. "New Jersey Admits 'Racial Profiling.'" *APBnews.com*, April 20, 1999. Accessed at http://www.apbnews.com/newscenter/breaking news/1999/04/20/profile0420_01.html.

Gratz et al. v. Bollinger et al. No. 97–75321 (E.D. Mich.) Ann Arbor: University of Michigan. Accessed at http://www.umich.edu/~urel/admissions/legal/expert/gurinapb.html.

Gravacs, Jenny. "Your Health." *Industry Week*, Oct. 7, 1996, pp. 94–100.

Greene, Jay P. "Why School Choice Can Promote Integration." *Education Week*, April 12, 2000, p. 52.

Greene, Jay P., and Nicole Mellow. "Integration Where It Counts: A Study of Racial

Integration in Public and Private School Lunchrooms." Paper presented at the meeting of the American Political Science Association, Boston, Sept. 1998.

Greens, Elizabeth. "Most Colleges Require Diversity Education." *Chronicle of Higher Education*, Nov. 3, 2000, p. A16.

Grieco, Margaret. *Keeping It in the Family: Social Networks and Employment Chance.* New York: Travistock, 1987.

Griffin, E., and G. G. Sparks. "Friends Forever: A Longitudinal Exploration of Intimacy in Same-Sex Pairs and Platonic Pairs." *Journal of Social and Personal Relationships* 7 (1990): 29–46.

Grodzins, Morton. "Metropolitan Segregation." *Scientific American* 197 (Oct. 1957): 33–41.

Grutter et al. v. Bollinger et al. No. 97–75928 (E.D. Mich.). Ann Arbor: University of Michigan. Accessed at http://www.umich.edu/~urel/admissions/legal/expert /gurinapb.html.

Guerrero, Laura, and Walid Affifi. "Some Things Are Better Left Unsaid: Topic Avoidance in Family Relationships." *Communication Quarterly* 43 (1995): 276–96.

Guthrie, Victoria L., Patricia King, and Carolyn Palmer. "Higher Education and Reducing Prejudice: Research on Cognitive Capabilities Underlying Tolerance." *Diversity Digest*, Spring/Summer 2000. Accessed at http://www.diversityweb.org /Digest/Sp.Sm00/contents.html.

Harlan, Megan. "Review of *Into the Tangle of Friendship*, by Beth Kephart." *New York Times Book Review*, Oct. 1, 2000, p. 18.

Harris, Sarah, and Ron Katsuyama, Report by the Social Science Research Center at the University of Dayton for the Dayton Region of the National Conference, 1996. A description of the key results of the report can be found in a January 16, 1997, University of Dayton press release at http://www.udayton.edu/news /nr/011797.html.

Herring, Cedric, and Charles Amissah. "Advance and Retreat: Racially Based Attitudes and Public Policy." Pp. 121–143 in *Racial Attitudes in the 1990s Continuity and Change*, ed. Steven A. Tuch and Jack K. Martin. Westport, CT: Praeger, 1997.

Herrnstein, Richard, and Charles Murray. *The Bell Curve.* New York: Free Press, 1994.

Heumann, Leonard. "The Definition and Analysis of Stable Racial Integration: The Case of West Mount Airy, Philadelphia." Ph.D. diss., University of Pennsylvania, Philadelphia, 1973.

Hitchcock, Jeff. *Unraveling the White Cocoon.* Dubuque, IA: Kendall/Hunt.

Hohman, Kimberly. "Coke Settles Discrimination Suit." *About.com*, Nov. 2000. Accessed at http://racerelations.about.com/newsissues/racerelations/library/weekly /aa112000a.htm.

Hooten, Katie. "Hotel Chain to Pay $8 Million to Settle Racial Bias Lawsuits." *Newsbytes*. Meeting Professionals International, TX, March 2000. 7, 13. Accessed at http://www.mpiweb.org/news/newsbytes/v713news.asp.

Hudson, J. Blaine, and Bonetta M. Hines-Hudson. "A Study of the Contemporary Racial Attitudes of Whites and African Americans." *Western Journal of Black Studies* 23, 1 (1999): 22–34.

Humphreys, Debra. "Campus Diversity and Student Self-Segregation: Separating Myths from Facts." Diversity Web: An Interactive Resource Hub for Higher Education, Association of American Colleges and Universities and the University of Maryland 1999. Accessed at http://www.diversityweb.org/Leadersguide/-

SED/studeseg.html. "Campus Diversity and Student Self-Segregation: Separating Myths from Facts." 1999. Accessed at http://www.diversityweb.org/Leadersguide/SED/studeseg.html.

"Improving the Collection and Use of Racial and Ethnic Data in HHS." Washington, D.C.: Department of Health and Human Services, 1999. Accessed at http://aspe.os.dhhs.gov/datacncl/racerpt/.

Jackman, Mary R., and Marie Crane. "'Some of My Best Friends Are Black . . .': Interracial Friendship and Whites' Racial Attitudes." *Public Opinion Quarterly* 50, 4 (1986): 459–86.

Jacobson, Jennifer. "In Brochures, What You See Isn't Necessarily What You Get." *Chronicle of Higher Education,* March 16, 2001, p. A41.

James, David R. "The Racial Ghetto as a Race Making Situation." In *Majority and Minority: The Dynamics of Race and Ethnicity in American Life,* ed. Norman R. Yetman. Boston: Allyn & Bacon, 1999.

Jerome, D. "Good Company: The Sociological Implications of Friendship." *Sociological Review* 32 (1984): 696–715.

Jones, Lisa Paynes. "Report of the Registrar: 1991–92 to 2000–01." Shaker Heights, OH: Shaker Heights City School District, 2000.

King, Marsha. "Nibbling Away at Racial Barriers." *Seattle Times,* Jan. 16, 2000. Accessed at http://seattletimes.nwsource.com/news/local/html98/race_20000116.html.

King, Mary-Claire. "Genomic Views of Human History." Keynote address at the HSC Poster Day, Kuwait University, April 23, 2001. Accessed at http://hscc.www.kuniv.edu.kw/poster/pages/keyspeak.htm.

Kinney, Janes. *Amalgamation!* Westport, CT: Greenwood Press.

Knapp, M. L. *Social Intercourse: From Greeting to Goodbye.* Boston: Allyn & Bacon, 1978.

Korgen, Kathleen. *From Black to Biracial.* Westport, CT: Praeger, 1999.

Korgen, Kathleen, and Jeffry Korgen. "From the 'One Drop Rule' to the Pigmentation Rule." *Southeastern Sociological Review* 1 (2000): 1–14.

Korgen, Kathleen, James Mahon, and Gabe Wang. "Diversity on College Campuses Today." *College Student Journal,* forthcoming.

Kory, Floyd. "Gender and Closeness Among Friends and Siblings." *Journal of Psychology* 129, 2 (1995): 193–202.

Krieger, Nancy. "Counting Accountably: Implications of the New Approaches to Classifying Race/Ethnicity in the 2000 Census." *American Journal of Public Health* November 2000, Vol. 90, No. 11, p. 1687.

Laertius, Diogenes. *Lives of the Philosophers* (Cambridge: Harvard University Press, 1969). Vol. 5, p. 25.

Landry, Bart. *The New Black Middle Class.* Berkeley: University of California Press, 1987.

Levine, Hillel, and Lawrence Harmon. *The Death of an American Jewish Community: A Tragedy of Good Intentions.* New York: Free Press, 1993.

Lipsitz, George. *The Possessive Investment in Whiteness.* Philadelphia: Temple University Press, 1998.

Lewis Mumford Center, "Ethnic Diversity Grows, Neighborhood Integration Lags Behind," *The Lewis Mumford Center for Comparative Urban and Regional Research,* April 3, Accessed at http://mumford1.dyndns.org/cen2000/report.html.

Marable, Manning. *Black Leadership*. New York: Columbia University Press, 1998.

Massey, Douglas S., and Nancy A. Denton. "The Construction of the Ghetto." Pp. 178–201 in *Majority and Minority: The Dynamics of Race and Ethnicity in American Life*, ed. Norman R. Yetman. Boston: Allyn & Bacon, 1999.

Matlock, John. "Student Expectations and Experiences: The Michigan Study." *Diversity Digest*, Summer 1997. Accessed at http://www.diversityweb.org/Digest/Sm97/contents.html.

McCall, George J., and J. L. Simmons. *Identities and Interactions*. New York: Free Press, 1978.

McIntosh, Peggy. "White Privilege: Unpacking the Invisible Knapsack." *Peace and Freedom*, July–Aug., 1989, pp. 10–12.

McWhirter, R. M., and J. D. Jecker. "Attitude Similarity and Inferred Attraction." *Psychonomic Science* 7 (1967): 225–26.

Mills, C. Wright. *The Sociological Imagination*. Oxford, Eng.: Oxford University Press, 1959.

Monsour, M., B. Harris, N. Kurzweil, and C. Beard. "Challenges Confronting Cross-Sex Friendships: 'Much Ado About Nothing?'" *Sex Roles* 31 (1994): 55–77.

Morin, Richard. "The Hidden Truth about Liberals and Affirmative Action." *The Washington Post*, Sept. 21, 1997, p. C5.

Morris, Lydia. "The Social Segregation of the Long-Term Unemployed in Hartlepool." *Sociological Review* 40 (1992): 344–69.

Nahemow, L., and M. P. Lawton. "Similarity and Propinquity in Friendship Formation." *Journal of Personality and Social Psychology* 32 (1975): 205–13.

Nemeth, C. "Differential Contributions of Majority and Minority Influence." *Psychological Review* 93 (1986): 23–32.

Newcomb, Theodore. "The Prediction of Interpersonal Attraction." *American Psychologist* 11 (1956): 575–86.

———. "Stabilities Underlying Changes in Interpersonal Attraction." *Journal of Abnormal and Social Psychology* 66 (1963): 376–86.

Newport, Frank, and Lydia Saad. "Civil Trial Didn't Alter Public's View of Simpson Case." *Gallup News Service*, Feb. 7, 1997. Accessed at http://www.gallup.com/poll/releases/pr970207.asp.

Nix, Jerry Vincent. "Assessing the Existence of Social Distance and Factors That Affect Its Magnitude at a Southern University," sspp.net vol. 1, 1997–1999. Accessed at http://www.sspp.net/archive/papers/nix.htm.

Noldon, Denise F., and William E. Sedlacek (1994). "A Comparison of Attitudes and Behaviors of Incoming Honors Freshmen by Race and Gender." Counseling Center, University of Maryland, College Park. Research Report # 4–94. Accessed at http://www.inform.umd.edu/EdRes/Topic/Diversity/General/Reading/Sedlacek/biggi.html.

"Noteworthy News: University of Idaho, Auburn U. Also Report Incidents of Doctored Photos." *Black Issues in Higher Education* (Oct. 26, 2000). Accessed at http://iibpchadwyck.com/toc/BlackIssuesinHigherEducation/26October2000.htm.

O'Brien, Eileen. *Whites Confront Racism: Antiracists and Their Paths to Action*. New York: Rowman & Littlefield, 2001.

Ojito, Mirta. "Best of Friends, Worlds Apart." *New York Times*, June 5, 2000, p. 1.

Orfield, Gary. "Schools More Separate: Consequences of a Decade of Resegregation." Cambridge, MA: Harvard University, 2001. Accessed at http://www.researchmatters.harvard.edu/story.php?article_id=268&section=society.

Park, Robert. Introduction to *The Marginal Man,* by Everett V. Stonequist. New York: Russell & Russell, 1937.

Parks, M. R., and K. Floyd. "Meanings for Closeness and Intimacy in Friendship." *Journal of Social and Personal Relationships* 13 (1996): 85–107.

Parrillo, Vincent. *Strangers to These Shores.* Boston: Allyn & Bacon, 2000.

Parrillo, Vincent, John Stimson, and Ardyth Stimson. *Social Problems.* Boston: Allyn & Bacon, 1999.

Pattillo-McCoy, Mary. *Black Picket Fences: Privilege and Peril Among the Black Middle Class.* Chicago: University of Chicago Press, 1999.

Pettigrew, Thomas F. "Generalized Intergroup Contact Effects on Prejudice." *Annual Review of Psychology* 49 (1997): 65–85.

———. "Intergroup Contact Theory." *Personality and Social Psychology Bulletin* 23, 2 (1998): 173–85.

Pine, Jordan. "Reach of School Segregation May Extend into the Future Workplace." *DiversityInc.com,* July 12, 2001. Accessed at http://www.diversityinc.com /public/department11.cfm.

Planalp, S., and A. Benson. "Friends' and Acquaintances' Conversations I: Perceived Differences." *Journal of Social and Personal Relationships* 9 (1992): 483–506.

Rawlins, W. K. *Friendship Matters: Communication, Dialectics, and the Life Course.* New York: Aldine de Gruyter, 1992.

Raybon, Patricia. *My First White Friend: Confessions on Race, Love, and Forgiveness.* New York: Penguin, 1996.

"Report of the Residential College Commission Subcommittee on Diversity." Rochester, NY: University of Rochester, 1999. Accessed at http://www.lib.Rochester.edu /diversity/divrep.htm.

Reskin, Barbara. *The Realities of Affirmative Action in Employment.* Washington, DC: American Sociological Association, 1998.

Robinson, Mary. "Tolerance and Diversity: A Vision for the 21st Century." Geneva, Switz.: United Nations High Commission for Human Rights, 2001. Accessed at http://www.parish-without-borders.net/cditt/jp/tolerance-unhchr.htm.

Rockwell, Paul. "The Right Has a Dream: Martin Luther King as an Opponent of Affirmative Action." *Extra!,* May/June 1995. Accessed at http://www.fair.org /extra/9505/king-affirmative-action.html.

Rosen, Jeffrey. "Without Merit." *New Republic,* May 14, 2001, p. 20.

Roth, Ann Macy. "Building Bridges to Afrocentrism," Jan. 26, 1995. Accessed at http://www.hartford-hwp.com/archives/30/134.html (originally distributed at ftp://oi.uchicago.edu/pub/papers/AMRoth_Afrocentrism.ascii.txt.)

Rothenberg, Paula. *Invisible Privilege: A Memoir About Race, Class, and Gender.* Lawrence: University Press of Kansas, 2000.

Saltman, Juliet. *A Fragile Movement: The Struggle for Neighborhood Stabilization.* Westport, CT: Greenwood Press, 1990.

Samter, Wendy, and William Cupach. "Friendly Fire: Topical Variations in Conflict Among Same and Cross-Sex Friends." *Communication Studies* 49, 42 (1998): 121–38.

Schelling, Thomas. *Micromotives and Macrobehavior.* New York: Norton, 1978.

Sedlacek, Bill. "Diversity Study 1995: Preliminary Summary of Results." *Institutional Profiles: Diversity Research and Evaluation.* College Park: University of

Maryland, 1995. Accessed at http://www.diversityweb.org/Profiles/divdbase/umd/DREI/1995_Survey_results.html.

Sias, Patricia, and Daniel J. Cahill. "From Coworkers to Friends: The Development of Peer Friendships in the Workplace." *Western Journal of Communication* 62, 3 (1998): 273–99.

Siebert, Darcy Clay, Elizabeth J. Mutran, and Donald C. Reitzes. "Friendship and Social Support: The Importance of Role Identity to Aging Adults." *Social Work* 44, 6 (1999): 522–33.

Smith, Tom W. "Trendlets: A. Inter-Racial Friendships." *GSS News*, May 2001. Accessed at http://www/icpsr.umich.edu/GSS/about/news/trenda.htm.

Southern Poverty Law Center, "Hate Goes to School," *Intelligence Report*, Spring 2000. Accessed at http://www.splcenter.org/cgi-bin/goframe.pl?refname=/intelligence project/ip-arch.html.

Steinberg, Stephen. *The Ethnic Myth*. Boston: Beacon Press, 1989.

Steinhorn, Leonard. "Martin Luther King's Half-Won Battle." *Ace Magazine*, Feb. 2000. Accessed at http://www.aceweekly.com/acemag/backissues/000202/cb000202.html.

Steinhorn, Leonard, and Barbara Diggs-Brown. *By the Color of Our Skin: The Illusion of Integration and the Reality of Race*. New York: Putnam, 2000.

Tatum, Beverly Daniel. "The ABC Approach to Creating Climates of Engagement on Diverse Campuses." *Liberal Education* 86, 4 (2000): 22–30.

———. *"Why Are All the Black Kids Sitting Together in the Cafeteria?"* New York: Basic Books, 1997.

Thernstrom, Stephan, and Abigail Thernstrom. *America in Black and White: One Nation, Indivisible*. New York: Simon & Schuster, 1997.

Thompson, Monita C., Teresa Graham Brett, and Charles Behling. "Educating for Social Justice: The Program on Intergroup Relations, Conflict, and Community at the University of Michigan." Pp. 99–114 in *Intergroup Dialogue*, ed. David Schoem and Sylvia Hurtado. Ann Arbor: University of Michigan Press, 2001.

Tinsley, Adrian. "A Vision for Bridgewater State College: Diversity." Bridgewater, MA: Bridgewater State College, 2001. Accessed at http://www.bridgew.edu/President/Vision.

Tuch, Steven A., Lee Sigelman, and Jack K. Martin. "Fifty Years After Myrdal: Blacks' Racial Policy Attitudes in the 1990s." Pp. 226–237 in *Racial Attitudes in the 1990s*, ed. Steven A. Tuch and Jack K. Martin. Westport, CT: Praeger, 1997.

Tucker, William H. *The Science and Politics of Racial Research*. Urbana: University of Illinois Press, 1994.

Turner, Judy, Miroslava Lhotsky, Peggy Edwards. *The Healthy Boomer*. Toronto: McClelland & Steward/Tundra, 2000.

Turner, Patricia. *I Heard It Through the Grapevine: Rumor in African American Culture*. Berkeley: University of California Press, 1992.

U.S. Bureau of the Census. "Black Population in the United States, March 1997." *Current Population Reports*, pp. 20–508. Washington, DC: U.S. Government Printing Office.

U.S. Department of Energy. "From the Genome to the Proteome: Basic Science." Oak Ridge, TN: U.S. Department of Energy Office of Biological and Environmental Research, n.d. Accessed at http://www.ornl.gov/hgmis/project/info.html.

Valia, Matthew. "Cultural Disconnect: How Whites, Blacks View Race in America." *DiversityInc.com,* July 10, 2001. Accessed at http://www.diversityinc.com/insidearticlepg.cfm?SubMenuID = 330&ArticleID = 3387&CFIL.

Walton, Anthony. "Technology Versus African-Americans." *Atlantic Monthly,* Jan. 1999, pp. 14–18. Accessed at http://www.theatlantic.com/issues/99jan/aftech.htm.

Wang, Gabe, and Kathleen Korgen. "Social Distance and College Students at a Northern New Jersey University." Pp. 95–107 in *The Quality of Contact: African Americans and Whites on College Campuses,* ed. Robert Moore. New York: University Press of America, 2002.

Waters, Mary C. *Black Identities: West Indian Immigrant Dreams and American Realities.* Cambridge, MA: Harvard University Press, 1999.

Welkos, Robert W., and Richard Natale. "Multiethnic Movies Ringing True with Youths." *Los Angeles Times,* June 2, 2001, p. A1. Accessed at http://www.latimes.com/news/state/20010702/t000054597.html.

Wiggins, James, Beverly Wiggins, and James Vander Zanden. *Social Psychology.* New York: McGraw-Hill, 1994.

Will, George F. "Dropping the 'One Drop' Rule." *Newsweek,* March 25, 2002, p. 64.

Williams, Jenny. "Redefining Institutional Racism." *Ethnic and Racial Studies* 8 (1985): 323–48.

Williams, Lena. *It's the Little Things.* New York: Harcourt, 2000.

Williams, Patricia J. *Seeing a Color-Blind Future: The Paradox of Race.* London: Virago Press, 1997.

Wilson, William Julius. "Affirming Opportunity," *American Prospect* 10, 46 (Sept.–Oct. 1999). Accessed at http://www.prospect.org/print/V10/46/wilson-w.html.

———. *The Declining Significance of Race.* Chicago: University of Chicago Press, 1978.

Index

About the Author

KATHLEEN ODELL KORGEN is Assistant Professor of Sociology at William Patterson University in Wayne, New Jersey. She has published several books and articles, including *From Black to Biracial: Transforming Racial Identity Among Americans* (Praeger).